Discovering
Stage Lighting

Discovering Stage Lighting

Second edition

Francis Reid

ELSEVIER
BUTTERWORTH
HEINEMANN

Focal
Press

AMSTERDAM • BOSTON • HEIDELBERG • LONDON • NEW YORK • OXFORD
PARIS • SAN DIEGO • SAN FRANCISCO • SINGAPORE • SYDNEY • TOKYO

Focal Press
An imprint of Elsevier
Linacre House, Jordan Hill, Oxford OX2 8DP
200 Wheeler Road, Burlington, MA 01803

First published 1993
Reprinted 1993, 1996, 1998
Second edition 1998
Reprinted 2000
Transferred to digital printing 2004

Permissions may be sought directly from Elsevier's Science & Technology Rights
Department in Oxford, UK: phone: (+44) 1865 843830, fax: (+44) 1865 853333,
e-mail: permissions@elsevier.co.uk. You may also complete your request on-line via
the Elsevier homepage (http:/www.elsevier.com), by selecting 'Customer Support'
and then 'Obtaining Permissions'

British Library Cataloguing in Publication Data
A catalogue record for this book is available from the British Library

Library of Congress Cataloguing in Publication Data
A catalogue record for this book is available from the Library of Congress

ISBN 0 2405 1545 5

For information on all Newnes publications
visit our website at www.newnespress.com

Printed and bound in Great Britain by Lightning Source UK Ltd

Contents

Prologue

Light has always been at the core of the actor's environment, and developing technology enables this light to be manipulated in an increasingly creative way. Used sympathetically, light supports the actors; used crudely, it may leave them cruelly exposed. How can we develop our ability to use light as a positive aid to communication with an audience?

While the spoken and written word can convey technical and organizational information, visual ideas are difficult to express in verbal form. Consequently, practical handling of light, with observation of the relation between effect and cause, is central to any study of stage lighting.

Work on the conceptual design of the lighting for a production, and the realization of that lighting design for performance to an audience, will always be the major learning situation. But the nature of preparing for a performance imposes considerable restriction on the extent to which it can be structured to provide optimum benefit to students: it is inevitable that the pressures of tight scheduling will accord a low priority to making time available for experiment or even for discussion. Laboratory-type projects allow students to be placed in situations which pose specific lighting problems, particularly those arising from the interaction of conflicting visual aims.

The core of this book is a series of discovery exercises which I have developed over the last thirty years while teaching lighting courses around the world.

Preliminary chapters support the projects within the context of a study of stage lighting fundamentals. Students are encouraged towards a systematic observation of light in nature and in art. Equipment is approached in a spirit of discovery, stimulated by question lists which identify the relevant points for experiment. In discussing the lighting design process, emphasis is placed on the self-questioning which leads to decision making.

Emphasis throughout the book is on discovery. It assumes that students should be encouraged to look, relate effect with cause, and make decisions. They should only be presented with facts when these will lead towards a constructive and safe use of time.

Photographs have been used only to identify equipment: students should be encouraged to find, and possibly collect, their own images of light in nature, art and the theatre.

Prologue to second edition

While the fundamentals of light and the basic aims and processes of lighting design remain constant, technology continues to advance. In particular, this new edition offers an opportunity to include material on the spotlights which have been developed to take advantage of the latest high-efficiency lamps which consume less electrical power but give more light.

Although automated spotlights are still expensive, their cost effectiveness for lighting management and their dynamic possibilities for lighting design ensures a growing absorption into standard practice. While few people using this book as a guide to discovery are likely to have access to these automated lights, their availability seems certain to increase during the currency of this edition. Certainly, any 'discoverer' attending a performance where automated lights are in use will wish to consider their effectiveness: consequently the analysis agendas have been expanded to include this new technology. Notes have been added to the projects where it might be interesting to experiment with automated lights if available. But, in the spirit of walking before running, such experiments should take place after the project has been fully explored with conventional equipment.

Three additional projects, developed at the National Theatre School of Canada in Montreal and the Bundesakademie für Kulturelle Bildung in Wolfenbüttel, have been placed at the end – not because they are more difficult but to retain a common numbering for groups using both the first and second editions.

For the equipment illustrations, the author is indebted to ADB, Compulite, ETC, M&M, Rosco, Selecon, Strand Lighting, Teatro, Ushio and Vari-Lite.

Part One
Fundamentals

1
Discovering light

The response of a theatre audience to stage lighting is influenced by experiences of light in the environment of their daily lives. They are also conditioned by the way light is used in the still images of paintings and photographs, and in the moving images of cinema and video. Much of this response is subconscious. Audiences rarely analyse stage lighting in a conscious way – unless the performance fails to hold their attention or they are students of lighting design. Apart from the irritation of just not being able to see detail, audience response to stage lighting is likely to take the form of a feeling of general visual unease that something is not quite right. This will also be the initial response of most of the production team of director, choreographer, designers and other specialists. However, unlike the audience, they will try to analyse their visual response in words, with the lighting designer as possibly the most articulate member of the team and certainly the person who has to find and implement a solution.

Anyone using light on the stage – particularly lighting designers but including everyone involved in the production team – needs to develop an awareness of the behaviour of light in a natural environment and the way that light is handled in various media. This is not so much a matter of formal study as a continuous informal response to the world around. The major equipment of lighting designers is their eyes: everything else is subsidiary.

Light in nature

The natural light by which we live is sourced by sun, moon and stars, augmented when necessary by artificial light from electric lamps. Most of this light is distributed by reflection from the various surfaces in our environment. It therefore tends to be softly diffuse and all-pervading. Some light may have a directional feel and this is particularly strong when natural light is channelled through such structures as windows, buildings and trees. The direction of this natural light changes within daily and seasonal cycles. Artificial sources tend to impart a directional feel by highlighting objects or people close to them.

The colour of natural light is dependent to some extent upon the atmosphere through which it travels: this may filter it and, under certain conditions, act as a prism to break it up. But the strongest influence comes from the colour of reflective surfaces. The tinting of daylight or artificial light by these methods is mostly subtle, with the possible exception of prismatic sunsets and strong sunlight filtered through leafy trees. Convention holds that the moon is blue and highly directional – and the words of many songs support this. However, in reality, it tends to be grey and all-pervading except when channelled through buildings. The blueness is largely an illusion stemming from the surrounding darkness.

Lighting designers tend to be more than normally aware of subtle shifts in direction, colour and balance of light outside and indoors. Student lighting designers are usually consciously aware but, with experience, this gradually becomes a subconscious awareness except when something jars the eye.

Awareness of light in the environment has an important role in the process of discovering light. Points to observe and consider in the course of one's daily life include:

Outside
■ sources, natural and artificial
■ directional quality, whether straight from source or channelled through structural features of the natural or built environment
■ effect of any filtering, e.g. by passing through foliage or mist, on texture and colour
■ colour of light from source
■ colour of reflective surfaces
■ resultant colour of reflected light
■ effect of direct light on environment surfaces
■ effect of indirect light on environment surfaces.

Inside
■ externally sourced light penetrating through windows, doors, etc.
■ directional quality of externally sourced light, including consequence of channelling through doors, windows, etc.
■ effect of reflective surfaces in distributing this externally sourced light
■ internal artificial light sources
■ directional quality of internally sourced artificial light arising from position of source
■ colour of light from external and internal sources
■ colour of reflective surfaces
■ resultant colour of reflected light.

Light in art

Study of painted, photographed and sculpted images is an important way of developing an understanding of the behaviour of light and a sensitive approach to its possibilities.

When painting three-dimensional images on two-dimensional canvas, the artist is dependent upon balance of light and shade to provide depth. It is interesting to study painting where the light source is included and the contrasts are strong and obvious, and then to look at paintings where there is no source, considering the directional quality of the light and its apparent source. Painters use light with varying degrees of subtlety. Occasionally they depict the actual light beam but more usually just its effect. Paintings can be particularly helpful in understanding reflections and the colour imparted to light by a reflective surface.

Photographers use light to strengthen the depth of image. They may do this deliberately, although the technology of the camera tends to strengthen contrasts automatically. Light and shade are particularly important in providing depth in monochrome photography whereas, in colour photography, the colour contrasts provide considerable depth.

Both painter and photographer use contrast and colour in light to create every kind of atmosphere from idyllic relaxation to creative tension. Study of a wide selection of portraits will reveal the subtle complexities of the response of facial structure and skin texture to light. Such a study will also demonstrate the way in which light and shade can enhance the fabric and cut of costumes. Landscapes will reveal how various individuals perceive light and use it to explore an environment in every possible style from heightened realism through varying degrees of impressionism to total symbolism.

The best approach is just to wander through galleries and look. Although accessible local collections may be short on acclaimed masterpieces, they can still be full of images to provide stimulation for both conscious critical analysis and subconscious response. Study of reproductions is, of course, also productive. But reproductions, however perfect, can never provide quite the same contact as the painter's canvas or the print from the photographer's own darkroom. When looking at artists' images, points for consideration include:

- apparent light sources, natural and artificial
- directional quality of the light, whether or not sources are included
- colour of light from sources
- colour of reflective surfaces
- resultant colour of reflected light
- effect of direct and indirect light on surfaces
- extent to which contrasts of light and shade may have been strengthened or distorted to increase the illusion of depth and three-dimensional modelling within the two-dimensional medium.

Sculptured objects help us to understand the way in which light reveals form. All three-dimensional objects, whether those of everyday life or works of art, provide us with a way of studying the effect of directional light using simple equipment like flashlights and adjustable desk lamps.

Light in film and video

Film and video makers take the manipulation of light a step further. In addition to revealing form and supporting atmosphere, the light contributes to the fourth-dimensional progression of time.

When studying moving image recordings, a stage lighting designer should concentrate on results rather than methods. The technical eye of a camera lens behaves in a different way to the human eye, particularly in its response to contrast. Perhaps the most rewarding study is black and white movies where the lighting cameraman has set up each individual shot for perfect pictorial composition, including a light balance sufficiently exaggerated to maximize light's potential for inserting depth into a basically flat medium. At the other end of the scale, much of today's video is shot under soft all-over lighting with a reliance for depth on general backlight plus differentiation in colour toning between the costumes and the scenic background. Note also the difference between the quality of light in images projected on white cinema screens and those displayed on video screens. Points for consideration include:

■ apparent light sources, natural and artificial
■ directional feel to the light, whether or not the source is included
■ use of contrasts of light and shade to increase the illusion of picture depth and the three-dimensional modelling of objects and people within the picture
■ use of contrasts of colour to separate actor from environment and increase the illusion of picture depth.

Light in the theatre

The fundamental requirement of light in the theatre is to illuminate the actors so that they are visible to the audience in all parts of the auditorium. If an actor is not fully visible at a particular moment, this should be as a result of a deliberate decision taken for dramatic effect. It must not happen by default.

The precise nature of this illumination may vary according to the type of performance. Faces in a spoken play, particularly eyes, are very important for character projection and audience contact. However, detailed facial expression may be less important in romantic nineteenth-century opera where the strain of producing beautiful sounds may be alien to the emotions being expressed. In dance, full illumination of the body is of prime importance. The possibility of controlling visibility at all parts of the stage is at the heart of stage lighting design.

Simple visibility can be achieved by throwing light on to actors and scenery from the front at a near horizontal angle. But such a light will flatten not only individual actors and pieces of scenery but also the composition of the stage picture, and will cast distracting shadows. The light that reveals should also sculpt. It should enhance the sculptural quality of the pictorial composition and of the individual actors and scenery within that picture. As the size of a conventional end-staged theatre increases, particularly one with a proscenium frame, the need for sculptural lighting increases in order to reduce the tendency towards a two-dimensional picture.

Therefore, although there are very few generalizations to be made about light on the stage, it is reasonably safe to assume that a primary requirement is sculptural visibility. Any departure from this should be for a very positive reason.

The extent to which light contributes in other ways will depend upon the lighting style chosen for a particular production. Light inevitably imposes some degree of selectivity upon audience vision and it influences the general atmosphere. This influence may be minimal or may extend to a major role in the way in which visual imagery is used to assist actors to communicate the work of writers and composers to an audience. The range of options for influencing an audience's visual priority is virtually limitless, from almost imperceptibly delicate shifts in balance to picking out areas from surrounding blackness by tightly shuttered spotlighting. Similarly, atmosphere, whether generated by contrasted light and shade or by colour, can be delicately or broadly indicated. This range of possible contrast in both selectivity and atmosphere not only applies within the 'frozen moment' of a static picture but is a feature of the changing pictures during the time sequence of a performance. These may vary from changes which are jarringly obvious to those so imperceptible that the audience are only subconsciously aware of them. A further major influence on lighting style is the extent to which the light on the stage endeavours to relate to the behaviour of the natural and artificial light in our daily environment. Again the options are wide, provided that the light relates visually to the rest of the stage picture and does not contradict the text. The key to style is consistency.

The primary decision area in lighting design is finding a credible answer to the question 'What contribution will light make to this production?' As we have noted, the answer will almost certainly include sculptural visibility. It may involve selection of areas and/or atmospheric support in all sorts of ways. It may well involve special effects and will certainly need to consider the extent of its conformity with the behaviour of light in nature.

When attending performances, it is inevitable that students of lighting design will concentrate much of their attention on observing and analysing the light. However, it is very important that they try not to think exclusively about lighting. Light means nothing on its own and is only valid in the context of the whole production. In observing stage lighting and its interaction with all other creative factors, the following points of interest are likely to emerge:

- adequacy of the sculptural visibility and its appropriateness for the type of performance
- balance of light levels between individual actors
- balance of light between individual elements in the scenic environment
- balance of light between the actors and their scenic environment
- use of light to focus audience attention
- use of light and shade to create atmosphere
- use of colour to create atmosphere
- light changes which are obvious to the audience
- light changes which the audience are not consciously aware of
- extent to which the light appears to be motivated by natural sources or visible artificial lighting fixtures
- extent to which the light appears to be motivated by directional sources which, although positive, are not identified with natural or artificial light
- any shadows which are distractingly illogical
- any light which is visually disturbing
- any use of a break-up texture in the light
- consequences, positive and negative, of light reflecting off surfaces, particularly the floor
- any effects, including projection
- any use of follow spots
- consistency in the way in which light is used throughout the production

2
Discovering lighting equipment

Lighting equipment manufacturers publish technical specification sheets with data on the operational characteristics of each item in their range. Although this information tends to be presented in the enthusiastically uncritical language of the marketplace, it forms an important reference on the shelves of every lighting designer's working library. However, no data sheet is a substitute for hands-on discovery of how a piece of equipment performs – particularly its performance in the real situation of an acting space rather than in a showroom or on an exhibition stand. Whether the equipment be spotlight, filter or control, the key to discovering its possibilities is hands-on observation, noting the relationship between effect and cause.

Light sources

Lighting instruments are devices which allow a lighting designer to control the emissions from a light source. The standard source of light for today's stage is the tungsten halogen lamp (Figure 2.1), which has several particularly relevant characteristics:

- It is dimmable by electrical means.
- It has a small glass envelope and a compact filament appropriate for inclusion within an efficient optical design.
- The initial light intensity is maintained throughout its life. (Filament particles which gradually blacken the glass envelope of simple tungsten lamps are returned to the filament by halogen gases.)

Most tungsten halogen lamps used in theatre have a compact filament which approximates as closely as is feasible to the optical ideal of a point source. A few lamps, used when a wide angled flood of light is required, have a long linear filament. Lamps normally operate on the local standard supply voltage with the result that, for stage lighting purposes, the world is divided into two: 220/240 volts and 110/120 volts. Lower voltage lamps give more light than higher voltage lamps of the same wattage, but the extra current drawn by the lower voltage requires much thicker cable. The final decade of the twentieth century has seen the introduction of a range

Figure 2.1 Some of the tungsten halogen lamps which provide the light source for theatre lighting instruments

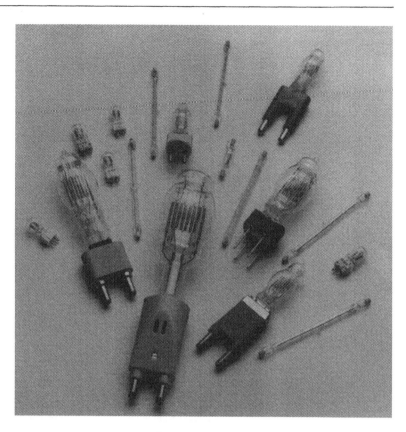

of lower-wattage high-efficiency halogen lamps using new compact filament structures and incorporating a heat sink in the base to dissipate the high temperature. The first lamp of this new generation to make an impact on stage lighting technology was the 575 W HPL (Figure 2.2). This has been followed by others such as the 600 W GKV and the Blue Pinch 1 kW.

For a particularly intense light, lamps of a much lower voltage, usually 24 volts, are sometimes used despite the inconvenience of including a transformer's weight and bulk within the instrument casing. However, this situation is likely to ease as larger capacity electronic transformers are developed. For some situations it is possible to take advantage of the high light output of low voltage lamps by connecting them in a series chain so that their total combined voltage equates with the supply.

For a really high intensity light, discharge types of lamp are available. These are the modern equivalent of the old carbon arc which generated light when electricity bridged the air gap between two carbon rods. In today's discharge lamps, the arc spans the gap between metallic electrodes enclosed with special gases in a quartz glass envelope. The types most commonly used in theatres are compact source iodine (CSI), compact iodide discharge (CID) and hygerium metallic iodide (HMI). The critical feature of discharge lamps is that they cannot be dimmed smoothly to blackout by electrical means but need mechanical shutters, operated either by hand or by remotely controlled motors.

Figure 2.2 575 HPL Compact
filament lamp with integral heat
sink

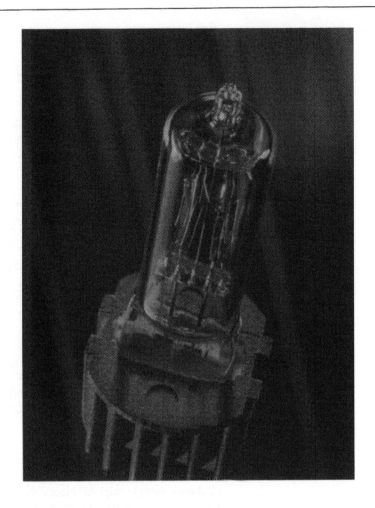

Lighting instruments

While data sheets provide basic information on such easily quantifiable
matters as light output and beam angle, lighting designers are particularly
concerned with the quality of the light and the speedy precision with which
beam size, shape and edge softness can be adjusted. Projecting light over
short throw distances on to white walls in a laboratory provides
information that is not only limited but so removed from the reality of the
stage that it is likely to be misleading. Experiment is required over a wide
range of the typical throw distances for which the instrument is likely to be
used. Lens adjustments, while providing satisfactory variations in beam
size and quality on long throws, may be inadequate at short range – and
vice versa. Moreover, light tends to hit scenery, actors and the floor at an
oblique angle. A plain white wall is the worst condition: most surfaces in
a stage performance are tinted and textured.

Therefore, when experimenting with a lighting instrument to discover its
potential, it is important to project the light over various throw distances,
from assorted angles, and on to different textures. The effect of each focus
adjustment knob should be observed for a comprehensive permutation of
distance, angle and texture. The simplest spotlights have only one focus

knob, but the more sophisticated have several and these tend to interact: adjustment of one affects the others so that fine tuning of the light is dependent upon going to and fro between knobs.

When experimenting with a light, the essential questions are:

● Is the overall quality of the light across the beam smooth or uneven? Is this quality fixed or can it be adjusted?
● Is the intensity of the light uniform across the beam or is it brighter in the centre with a decrease towards the edge? Is this distribution of intensity across the beam fixed or can it be adjusted?
● Is the edge of the beam free from discoloration by a bluish ring?
● Can the quality of the edge be adjusted? If so, can it be easily softened without spoiling the quality of the light across the beam? Is there any tendency for lens adjustments to produce a double image when focused for soft edge?
● Does the instrument accept gobo patterns? If so, how sharp an image can be produced? Can this image be softened progressively and evenly until it is a barely discernible texture? Is the image even across the beam, whatever the focus?
● How can the beam be shaped: approximately with barndoors, or precisely with shutters? If barndoors, does the assembly rotate and do the individual blades remain firmly in the desired position? If shutters, can they be angled easily and/or does the shutter assembly rotate?
● What is the possible variation, from maximum to minimum, in beam angle? Does the light fall off significantly in intensity or quality towards either or both extremes of this beam angle range? If so, what is the practical beam variation consistent with achieving a good light?
● Are the adjustment devices mechanically reliable? Do they move easily and smoothly? Do they lock positively?
● Is the instrument safe (electrically and mechanically)?
● How easy is maintenance (cleaning and mechanics)?

Types of lighting instruments

There is no single universal lighting instrument which will do everything. A lighting designer has to choose appropriate instruments for each requirement in each production. But decisions are not made on the grounds of art alone. Budgets and schedules are a major influence:

● What can we afford to rig?
● How much technical stage time do we have for focusing?

Frequently, the matter of choice is narrowed to making the best use of whatever equipment is available: determining priorities is a major lighting design skill.

Most decision processes are simplified by breaking down the areas of choice into subsections. Lighting instruments break down into a series of families, with groups and subgroups within these families.

Floods

Figure 2.3 International symbol for floods

As the name suggests, floods provide a general wash of light. The traditional flood is a box with a round lamp and reflector (Figures 2.3, 2.4). Like all stage lighting instruments, the box has an up/down tilting

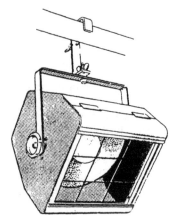

Figure 2.4 A traditional flood

mechanism and may be panned left/right at the point of suspension. There are no other adjustments such as focus knobs: the size of area lit and the light quality result from the throw distance and the type of flood chosen. To light a larger or smaller area, the flood must be moved further away or brought closer. The general quality of the beam depends on the design of the reflector and the degree of hardness of the beam edge is virtually accidental, depending upon the relationship between instrument casing, reflector and throw distance.

Symmetric floods

Most modern floods use a linear lamp to provide the wider beam at close range which is desirable when lighting large areas of sky or painted scenic cloths. Some linear floods have a reflector which gives a symmetric spread of light with height approximately the same as width (Figure 2.5). The middle of the beam tends to be more intense than its top and bottom.

Asymmetric floods

Most linear floods have an asymmetric reflector which is designed to extend the vertical spread in order to increase the coverage down a cloth at close range (Figure 2.6). The light has an even intensity across its beam.

Figure 2.5 Linear flood with symmetrical reflector (Strand Nocture)

Figure 2.6 Linear flood with asymmetrical reflector (Strand Coda)

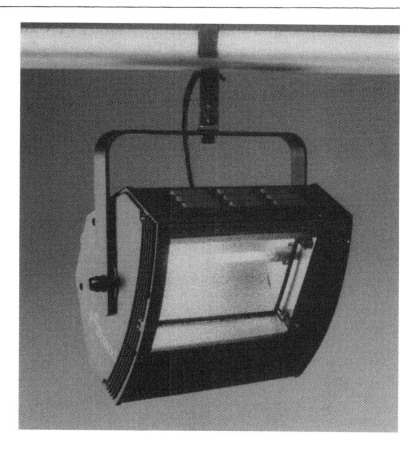

Experiment with all types of available flood on a wide range of throw distances, observing:

- size and shape of area lit
- quality of light, especially its general distribution and edge
- extent and smoothness of cover when lighting a large area of scenery (e.g. a cloth or a wall) at close range from both above and below.

Conical beam spotlights

Most spotlights have conical beams. Since the light emerges as a cone, the size of area lit increases with the throw distance. Knowing the angle of this cone, we can calculate the spread of the light for any throw distance, or calculate the angle required for a particular spread on a given throw (Figure 2.7). The angle of the light cone is usually called the 'beam angle', although strictly speaking it is the 'half peak angle', defined as the point in the distribution of light across the beam where intensity falls away to not less than half its maximum value. The human eye, however, perceives this as a virtually even beam – so the definition is more important to lighting engineers than to lighting designers.

PC focus spots

Conical beam spotlights vary in degrees of sophistication. The simplest type is the focus spot where lamp and reflector move in relation to a fixed planoconvex (PC) lens (Figures 2.8, 2.9, 2.10). As the light source moves

Figure 2.7 Beam diameters or spreads (metres) for ranges of beam angle and throw distance

Throw Distance

Beam Angle	3m	4m	5m	6m	7m	8m	9m	10m	11m	12m	13m	14m	15m	16m
4°	0.2	0.3	0.3	0.4	0.5	0.6	0.6	0.7	0.8	0.8	0.9	1.0	1.0	1.1
6°	0.3	0.4	0.5	0.6	0.7	0.8	0.9	1.0	1.2	1.3	1.4	1.5	1.6	1.7
8°	0.4	0.6	0.7	0.8	1.0	1.1	1.3	1.4	1.5	1.7	1.8	2.0	2.1	2.2
10°	0.5	0.7	0.9	1.0	1.2	1.4	1.6	1.7	1.9	2.1	2.3	2.4	2.6	2.8
12°	0.6	0.8	1.1	1.3	1.5	1.7	1.9	2.1	2.3	2.5	2.7	2.9	3.2	3.4
14°	0.7	1.0	1.2	1.5	1.7	2.0	2.2	2.5	2.7	2.9	3.2	3.4	3.7	3.9
16°	0.8	1.1	1.4	1.7	2.0	2.2	2.5	2.8	3.1	3.4	3.7	3.9	4.2	4.5
18°	1.0	1.3	1.6	1.9	2.2	2.5	2.9	3.2	3.5	3.8	4.1	4.4	4.8	5.1
20°	1.1	1.4	1.8	2.1	2.5	2.8	3.2	3.5	3.9	4.2	4.6	4.9	5.3	5.6
22°	1.2	1.6	1.9	2.3	2.7	3.1	3.5	3.9	4.3	4.7	5.1	5.4	5.8	6.2
24°	1.3	1.7	2.1	2.6	3.0	3.4	3.8	4.3	4.7	5.1	5.5	6.0	6.4	6.8
26°	1.4	1.8	2.3	2.8	3.2	3.7	4.2	4.6	5.1	5.5	6.0	6.5	6.9	7.4
28°	1.5	2.0	2.5	3.0	3.5	4.0	4.5	5.0	5.5	6.0	6.5	7.0	7.5	8.0
30°	1.6	2.1	2.7	3.2	3.8	4.3	4.8	5.4	5.9	6.4	7.0	7.5	8.0	8.6
32°	1.7	2.3	2.9	3.4	4.0	4.6	5.2	5.7	6.3	6.9	7.5	8.0	8.6	9.2
34°	1.8	2.4	3.1	3.7	4.3	4.9	5.5	6.1	6.7	7.3	7.9	8.6	9.2	9.8
36°	1.9	2.6	3.2	3.9	4.5	5.2	5.8	6.5	7.1	7.8	8.4	9.1	9.7	10.4
38°	2.1	2.8	3.4	4.1	4.8	5.5	6.2	6.9	7.6	8.3	9.0	9.6	10.3	11.0
40°	2.2	2.9	3.6	4.4	5.1	5.8	6.6	7.3	8.0	8.7	9.5	10.2	10.9	11.6
42°	2.3	3.1	3.8	4.6	5.4	6.1	6.9	7.7	8.4	9.2	10.0	10.7	11.5	12.3
44°	2.4	3.2	4.0	4.8	5.7	6.5	7.3	8.1	8.9	9.7	10.5	11.3	12.1	12.9
46°	2.5	3.4	4.2	5.1	5.9	6.8	7.6	8.5	9.3	10.2	11.0	11.9	12.7	13.6
48°	2.7	3.6	4.5	5.3	6.2	7.1	8.0	8.9	9.8	10.7	11.6	12.5	13.4	14.2
50°	2.8	3.7	4.7	5.6	6.5	7.5	8.4	9.3	10.3	11.2	12.1	13.1	14.0	14.9
52°	2.9	3.9	4.9	5.9	6.8	7.8	8.8	9.8	10.7	11.7	12.7	13.7	14.6	15.6
54°	3.1	4.1	5.1	6.1	7.1	8.2	9.2	10.2	11.2	12.2	13.2	14.3	15.3	16.3
56°	3.2	4.3	5.3	6.4	7.4	8.5	9.6	10.6	11.7	12.8	13.8	14.9	16.0	17.0
58°	3.3	4.4	5.5	6.7	7.8	8.9	10.0	11.1	12.2	13.3	14.4	15.5	16.6	17.7
60°	3.5	4.6	5.8	6.9	8.1	9.2	10.4	11.5	12.7	13.9	15.0	16.2	17.3	18.5

Beam Angle (left side) — *Beam Diameter (in metres)* (right side)

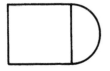

Figure 2.8 International symbol for PC focus spots

Figure 2.9 Section through basic optics of a PC focus spot

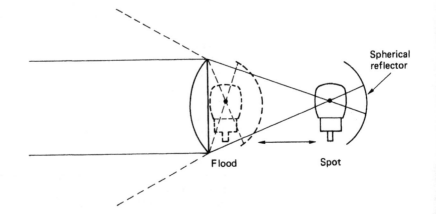

Spherical reflector

Flood   Spot

Figure 2.10 A 1.2 kW planoconvex
focus spot (Selecon PC 1200)

towards the lens, the angle of the conical beam of light emerging from the instrument increases. PC focus spots therefore offer a range of beam angles from a minimum 'spot' (lamp and reflector fully back) to a maximum 'flood' (lamp and reflector fully forward). This beam angle range varies with the design of the instrument, particularly its lens, but is typically from a minimum of around 4° to 8° up to a maximum of 50° to 60°.

While their beam size can be controlled positively, focus spots offer only primitive adjustments to their beam shape by the four flaps of a rotatable 'barndoor' shuttering device which can be fixed as an accessory to the front of the instrument casing.

Beam quality is dependent upon the lens used. The traditional clear PC lens has a hardish edge which tends to have a slight rainbow discoloration. However, most of today's lenses incorporate sufficient diffusion in their structure, usually by stippling the rear surface, to provide an edge that, although still positive, is slightly soft.

Fresnel spots

Fresnel spotlights are very similar to PC focus spots: the only difference is the lens which is stepped at the front and textured at the back (Figures 2.11, 2.12, 2.13). Fresnel lenses provide a light which is softer and has a much less well defined edge than that of the PC. They also tend to cast softer shadows. Fresnel beams do not narrow to quite such a small spot as PCs but they can open to a wider flood. Fresnel lenses produce quite considerable stray (or 'scatter') light outside their main beam and therefore, when used close to scenery, particularly borders, require barndoors to contain scatter in addition to roughly shaping the beam.

Figure 2.11 International symbol
for Fresnel spots

Figure 2.12 Section through basic optics of a Fresnel spot

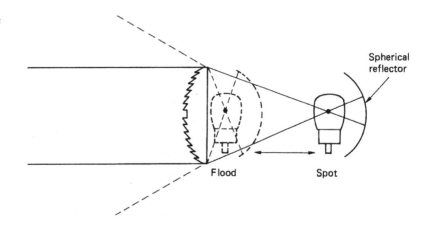

Spherical reflector

Flood   Spot

Figure 2.13 A 1.2 kW Fresnel spot (Selecon SF 1200)

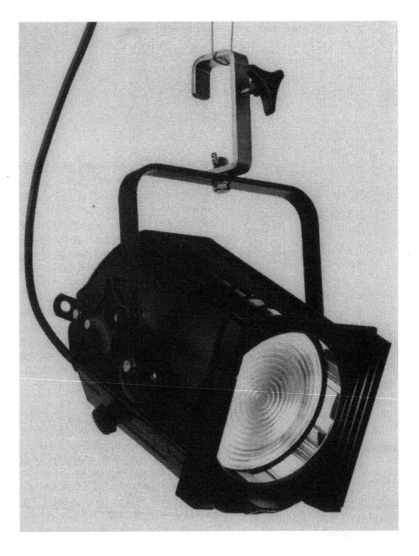

Experiment with various types of PC and Fresnel spotlights over alternative throw distances, comparing them and observing:

- the difference in light quality between PCs and Fresnels and between different makes of instruments
- the limits of their beam angles from narrowest spot to widest flood
- whether there is any deterioration in quality towards the extreme limits of fully spotted and fully flooded
- the relative degree of hardness/softness of shadows projected by actors/objects caught by the beam at different points within the throw
- the scatter of stray light outside the main beam, noting variations between different Fresnel instruments, particularly in relation to lens diameter
- the use of barndoors to limit this scatter
- the use of barndoors to shape the beam of both PCs and Fresnels.

Profile spots

The quality of the light, particularly its edge, is not controllable on either PC or Fresnel spotlights. And while there is positive adjustment of beam size, any shaping of the beam is rough and approximate. Selection of either of these types of instrument determines the light quality and the only possible change that may be made is by passing the light through a filter. For more precise control of the light beam, profile spots are appropriate.

The movements inside a profile spot are the opposite of those inside a PC or Fresnel: the lamp and reflector are static but the lens moves (Figures 2.14, 2.15). Profile spots have a more complex reflector, usually

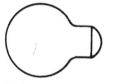

Figure 2.14 International symbol for profile spots

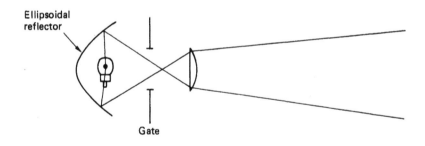

Figure 2.15 Section through basic optics of a profile spot

ellipsoidal, which collects the light at the optical system's critical point called the 'gate' where its size and shape can be manipulated. The beam can then be focused to the required degree of hardness or softness by moving the lens. Adjustments at the gate are made by a set of four shutter blades and/or by an iris diaphragm. In most models the iris is optional and inserted in a slot which will accept, alternatively, a two-dimensional mask known as a 'gobo' (Figure 2.16). Any outline shape cut in this gobo mask may then be projected, using the lens to control the sharpness of image. The name 'profile' is derived from the ability of this type of spot to project the profile of any object placed at the gate – whether shutter combination, iris or gobo. In North America, profile spots are usually referred to as 'ellipsoidals'. They are also frequently known as 'Lekos', a Century Inc. brand name which has become a generic term.

Although the lamp of a profile spot is not moved to vary the beam angle, most profiles have a knob which allows precise positioning of the lamp in

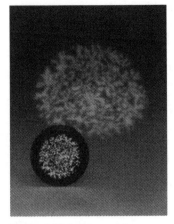

Figure 2.16 A gobo and its
projected pattern (Rosco)

relation to the reflector. This provides a fine tuning adjustment with the
option of either an even intensity across the beam, or a brighter peak in the
centre with a falling off towards the perimeter.

The lens of a profile spot determines its beam angle. Reducing the beam
angle for a smaller spread involves the use of shutters or iris and is an
inefficient process which converts light into heat. It is therefore important
to select an instrument with the correct beam angle for the area to be lit
(Figure 2.17). This is fine when equipment is rigged specially for a
production with a long run of performances, but is less satisfactory when
there are frequent changeovers.

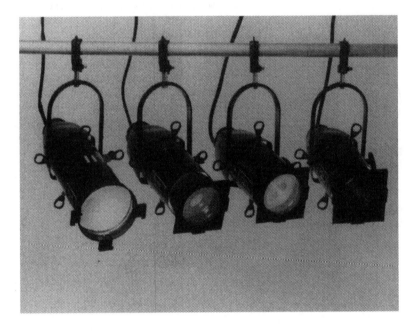

Figure 2.17 Profile spots with
lenses for alternative beam angles
(Strand Lekos)

Variable beam profile spots

Flexibility in permanent installations requires a more sophisticated profile
spot with a range of beam angles. These variable beam profile spots have
lamps, reflectors and gates identical to basic profile spots but use a zoom-
type arrangement of two lenses (Figures 2.18, 2.19, 2.20). However, unlike
the coupled zoom systems of cameras, the lenses in variable beam profiles
move independently to allow optional sharpness of image in addition to
variations in beam angle. Typical beam angle ranges are the 11/26°, 18/32°
and 26/44° of the Strand 1.2 kW Cantata.

Condenser optics

Some profile spots use a condenser lens between the lamp and the gate to
obtain a very even distribution of light over the gate area (Figure 2.23).
This provides the possibility of a very sharply defined profile of shutter, iris
or gobo.

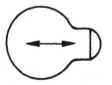

Figure 2.18 International symbol
for variable beam profile spots

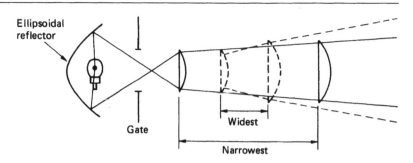

Figure 2.19 Section through basic optics of a variable beam profile spot

Figure 2.20 A 1.2 kW variable beam profile spot (Strand Cantata 18/32)

New generation profile spots

A general upgrading of many of the optical and mechanical features of traditional profile spots has been stimulated by the arrival of the new lower-wattage high-efficiency lamps. In particular, the use of a dichroic coating on the reflectors ensures a much-reduced temperature at the gate. This minimizes the tendency of intricate gobos to bend, thus providing a clean silhouette which does not become distorted after extended burning. The cool temperature also ensures that shutters are much less likely to become jammed as a result of expansion. The investment by most manufacturers in castings rather than the more usual extrusions or bent metal tends to provide an instrument which combines robustness with compact elegance (Figures 2.21, 2.22).

Experiment with various profiles, both basic and variable beam, over alternative throw distances, observing:
- the hard/soft focusing, noting the extent to which a change of focus also alters image size

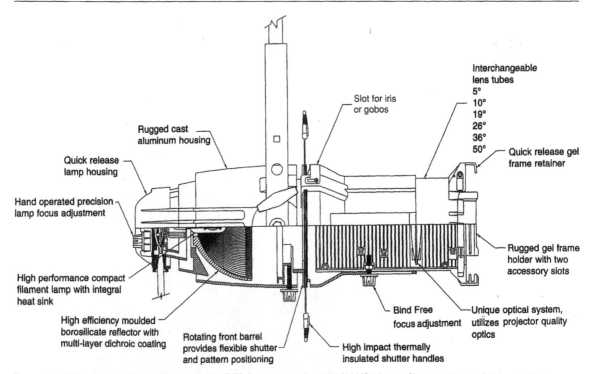

Rugged cast
aluminum housing

Quick release
lamp housing

Hand operated precision
lamp focus adjustment

High performance compact
filament lamp with integral
heat sink

High efficiency moulded
borosilicate reflector with
multi-layer dichroic coating

Rotating front barrel
provides flexible shutter
and pattern positioning

Slot for iris
or gobos

Interchangeable
lens tubes
5°
10°
19°
26°
36°
50°

Quick release gel
frame retainer

Rugged gel frame
holder with two
accessory slots

Bind Free
focus adjustment

Unique optical system,
utilizes projector quality
optics

High impact thermally
insulated shutter handles

Figure 2.21 New generation profile spotlight. (ETC Source 4, using 575 W HPL lamp. Six interchangeable lens tubes provide beam angles from 5° to 50°.) See also Figure 2.32 on page 28

Figure 2.22 New generation zoom profile spotlight. (Strand Brio, using 600 W GKV lamp. 18/30° or 25/50° beam angle options are available)

Figure 2.23 Section through basic optics of a variable beam profile spot with condenser optics (ADB)

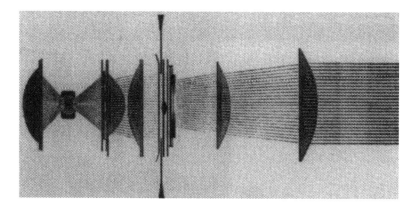

- the beam spread of variable beam profiles from their narrowest to their widest
- how focusing affects the light quality, including evenness of beam and any tendency to a double image of the edge, or possible discoloration of the edge by a bluish ring
- the interaction of beam size and quality between the two lenses of variable beam profiles
- the effect of adjusting the beam between even and peaky
- the potential of the shutters: endeavour to match beam shape to irregular objects
- how various gobos can be used to produce sharp images and then progressively defocused with the lens until the light is just slightly broken up with a delicate texture
- comparative light output from instruments using 1.2 kW lamps and those with the new 575 W or similar lamps
- differences in temperature at the gate, colour filter and body, particularly between instruments using standard reflectors and those with dichroic coated reflectors.

Parallel beams

The alternative to a conical beam is a parallel beam which will have the same spread whatever the throw. Such a beam is produced by a parabolic reflector and no lens.

Figure 2.24 International symbol for beamlights

Beamlights
Although lens systems provide control of light beams, they also reduce their intensity. The absence of lenses and the concentration of all the emitted light into a tightly parallel beam results in an intense light which tends to make its presence visible by the way in which it picks up any particles of moisture or dirt in the atmosphere. For this reason, such instruments are called 'beamlights' (Figures 2.24, 2.25, 2.26).

All light from the instrument must come from the reflector with no direct light from the lamp. Two alternative techniques are used to ensure this. Either a silvered reflector lamp is mounted through a hole in the centre of the reflector, or a small mirror is mounted in front of the lamp to block emission of any direct light and return it to the main reflector. In both cases, matt black spill rings are fitted to minimize scatter of stray light resulting from impurities or inaccuracies in reflector design or manufacture. A few

Figure 2.25 Section through basic optics of a beamlight

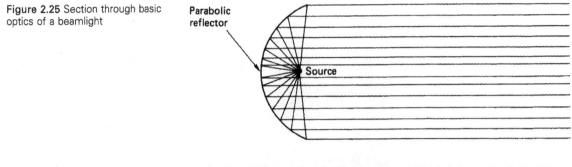

Figure 2.26 A 24 V 500 W beamlight (Strand Beamlite 500)

beamlights use standard tungsten halogen sources, but most have 24 volt lamps of either 500 or 1000 watts, with a transformer mounted inside the instrument casing.

Parcans

The parcan is the member of the parallel beam family in most common use. Par lamps, rather like motor car headlamps in appearance, include not just a filament but a complete optical system within their glass envelopes (Figure 2.28). The reflector is a near parabola and the front of the glass is moulded to give a small amount of diffusion. The reflector is slightly asymmetric so that the near parallel beam is slightly extended in one plane. Different par lamps offer different beams, complemented by appropriate strengths of diffusion. Par lamps are available at 110/120 and 220/240 volts, with the 120 volt types often paired in series on a 240 volt supply for extra intensity. The parcan is just that – a simple can with matt black interior. The only adjustment, apart form standard pan and tilt, is the possibility of twisting the lamp for orientation of its asymmetric beam. As

Figure 2.27 Source 4 PAR using the 575 HPL lamp and a set of four lenses which snap in to a rotating mount for alternative beam widths (ETC)

with other lights, smoke will increase the visibility of the beam (Figure 2.29).

New generation parcans

As an alternative to the sealed beam par lamp, the new 575 W lamp may be used with a moulded plastic lens (Figure 2.27). The light output is comparable with that of the 1 kW par lamp. Alternative lenses clip into the front of the can, permitting a fast change of beam angle.

Experiment with beamlights and parcans over alternative throw distances, observing:

For beamlights:
- how parallel the beam is
- quality of the beam, including the softness of its edge, and use of the lamp adjusting knob to keep the beam free from a central black spot
- extent to which the beam is visible in the air (compare with other types of instrument).

Figure 2.28 A 1 kW parcan (Strand
Punchlite)

Figure 2.29 Smoke increases the
visibility of light beams (M&M
Scotty Smoke Gun)

For parcans:
- size and shape of the beam from various types of par lamps
- quality of the beam, including smoothness across the beam and the softness of its edge
- comparative intensity of parcan and various conical beam lensed instruments of the same wattage
- extent to which the beam is visible in the air.

For new generation parcans:
- size and shape of the beam from alternative lenses
- quality of beam, including smoothness across the beam and the softness of its edge
- comparative intensity of new 'parcans' with standard parcans of a higher wattage
- extent to which the beam is visible in the air.

Follow spots

High-quality, low-voltage beamlights make good instruments for following actors discreetly at a relatively short range (perhaps up to about 10 metres). The transformer may be mounted separately, and the absence of lenses, whose movement would shift the centre of gravity, allows the instrument to be finely balanced. The edge is positive yet sufficiently indistinct not to attract notice, while the high-intensity parallel beam covers the actors neatly from head to waist at all parts of the stage without adjustment, allowing the operator to concentrate on precision following.

For long throws, profile spots are standard. Some softening of the edge is normal except for the more obvious style of following which emphasizes the status of a star. In all but the smallest studio stage situations, discharge lamps are used. Since any small shake is exaggerated over long throw distances, these follow spots need to be robust and firmly mounted on heavy stands. With an operator in attendance, the difficulties in fading discharge lamps are no problem: mechanical dimming can be as simple as a blackout card replacing one of filters in the hand-operated colour-change magazine.

Experiment with various follow spots (or with instruments with a potential for following) over alternative throw distances, observing:
- adjustments required to keep the beam at a constant size as actors move nearer and further away
- stability of the light so that it does not tremble
- ease with which beam edge can be softened and hardened
- ease with which colours can be changed.

Discharge lamp instruments

Profile spots with discharge lamps are sometimes used over long throws in large auditoriums. For dimming purposes they are fitted with motorized dimming shutters which are usually designed on the venetian blind principle. With the motor operated from a standard dimming channel, the operation of these lights can be coordinated with that of the rest of the lighting rig.

Figure 2.30 Motorized dimmer shutter fitted to Fresnel spotlight with high-intensity discharge lamp (Compulite Corona)

Powerful HMI discharge Fresnel spotlights, originally made for film and video studios, are finding increasing stage use as a clean powerful motivational source. A mechanical shutter, under human or motorized control, is necessary for dimming (Figure 2.30).

Other major uses for discharge lamps are in projectors (see section 'Effects' later in this chapter) and in some automated lights.

Automated lights

Spotlights which are focused by remotely controlled motors are not yet standard equipment. However, their use is increasing, particularly in situations where the capital costs are justified not only by their contribution to the quality of the lighting design but by gains in flexibility and safety, accompanied by savings in time and labour. As a design tool, automated focusing allows beams to move in sight of the audience while changing beam size, shape, quality and colour. As a management tool, instruments may be refocused between cues in a performance or between productions in a repertoire season.

Automated instruments come in two broad categories. The simplest (Figures 2.31, 2.32) is the addition of motors to standard equipment: most conventional 1.2 kW, 2 kW and 2.5 kW tungsten halogen spotlights can be provided with special suspension arms giving motorized pan, tilt and focus. More complex automated lights (Figure 2.33) use discharge lamps and

Figure 2.31 PC spotlight with
remote control motor drives for
pan, tilt and focus (Strand
Pirhouette)

include motorized mechanical dimming, focus, gobo library, and dichroic
filter wheels for unlimited colour mixing. There are two formats, known as
wash and *spot*, broadly corresponding to Fresnel and profile. In some types
of automated instrument, especially those used for the type of special
effects associated with discotheques, the instrument body is stationery with
pan and tilt of the beam controlled by a motorized mirror.

Experiment with any available automated lights, observing:

For lighting management:
- potential for refocusing after they have faded out in cues.

For dynamic movement while alight:
- shift of focus, either both boldly or delicately, from one part of the stage
  to another and from one actor to another
- wide beams narrowing as the attention tightens in on a solo actor

Figure 2.32 ETC Source 4 profile spotlight with colour scroller, mounted in a Compulite Mini Whisper modular yoke for remote pan and tilt

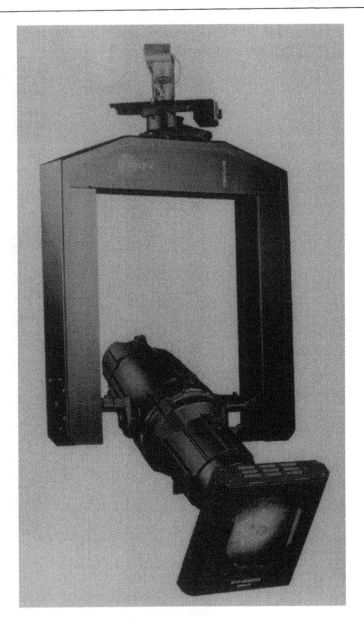

- narrow beams gradually opening out to reveal an increasingly wide area
- series of moving beams converging upon one person
- slow start and dramatic acceleration.

Filters

Filters offer a means of controlling the quality and colour of the light emerging from a lighting instrument. The filters are often referred to as 'gels' but it is some considerable time since coloured gelatine was used as a filter medium. Apart from its tendency to fade and become brittle, its use

Figure 2.33 Highly sophisticated automated spotlight with interchangeable wheels for gobos and dichroic colour mixing (Varilite VL6)

poses a degree of fire risk that is unacceptable in most parts of the world. Today's filters are made from polycarbonate or polyester material with dye either applied to the surface or sandwiched between two layers. Many of the filter ranges are designed to survive the higher temperatures and light intensities generated by the newer sources and optical systems.

Diffusion filters

Diffusion filters soften a light beam and this softening is, of course, particularly noticeable at the edge. As more delicate diffuser filters have become available, there has been a growing tendency to soften the beams of profile spotlights with these filters rather than by the traditional defocusing of the lens. Softening with a filter is much quicker, and defocusing tends to lose some of the intensity and even-beam quality which is produced by efficient modern optical systems with computer-designed reflectors. Diffusion filters, however, do tend to produce a certain amount of stray or scattered light and care has to be taken when lights are hung close to scenery or used on longer throws from the auditorium.

Some diffusers stretch the light in one plane in addition to softening it. These filters are called 'silks' because of the fine lines running through the material in one direction. However, silks do not stretch the light in the same direction as these lines but at 90° to them. The light emerging from the instrument can be stretched at any oblique angle by the way in which the filter is cut and framed.

Experiment with various diffuser and silk filters, observing:
- the effect on the beam
- any tendency to scatter light on scenery adjacent to the lens

using:

- a PC focus spot beam
- a Fresnel beam
- a hard focused profile beam
- symmetric and asymmetric floods.

Correction filters

Light emitted by each type of source has its own particular version of the spectrum. The 'whiteness' of white light is called 'colour temperature' and is measured on the Kelvin scale: the range is from 2600°K for white light with a high red content to 6000°K for white light with a high blue content. Most tungsten halogen lamps used in theatre are rated at about 3200°K, while the CSI discharge lamps used in many follow spots are 4000°K, but the difference is more critical for video and film cameras than for human eyes.

A range of correction filters is made for studio use, each with a stipulated purpose such as converting tungsten light to simulate daylight. While these filters are often used in theatre, this use tends to be based rather more on experimental observation than on strictly scientific principles. In particular, very pale grey steel tints are commonly used to increase the whiteness of white light in the same way that detergent manufacturers use blue to produce 'whiter than white'. Indeed this kind of corrective filtering was at the heart of Brecht's 'white light' clarity.

Experiment with various pale filters, including examples from the correction series, on a dimmable tungsten halogen light, observing:
- warming of an unfiltered tungsten halogen light as it is dimmed
- effect of various filters on the undimmed light
- filtering to compensate for the warming effect of dimming.

If any discharge lamps are available, observe:

- colour differences between tungsten halogen and available discharge lamps
- use of filters to correct these differences (in both directions).

Colour filters

Unfiltered light includes the entire colour spectrum. Filtering removes unwanted colours, emphasizing those that remain and thus 'colouring' the light. The fact that this colouring occurs by a subtraction process is a major factor in understanding the use of coloured light on the stage. For a lively vibrant response under light, any surface needs to receive the colours of the spectrum which correspond to all the pigments present in that surface. If some spectral colours are missing, the response of the surface, whether actor face, costume fabric or scenic material, will be distorted. Because deeply saturated filters subtract more of the spectrum than do the paler tints, there will be a tendency for that distortion to increase as the light becomes more positively coloured. The distorting effect of colour filtering can make a major contribution to the stage atmosphere, provided that the degree of distortion is rigidly controlled.

Experiment with a wide selection of filters to colour the light thrown simultaneously on to various coloured materials and flesh (perhaps a person wearing a multicoloured costume), observing:

- response of the various pigments to the light from each filter, noting where a filter enhances, changes or deadens
- response of flesh to the light from each filter, noting the acceptable depth of saturation before the face becomes unnatural
- different response between blue filters of similar saturation but passing light with a greater red or green content
- different response between warm filters of similar saturation but biased towards pinks, golds, ambers and yellows
- the colour of each filter when held up to a tungsten light compared with the effect of the filtered light on materials
- whether the filter's name is helpful or misleading (at worst it may be a marketing fantasy, at best an over-simplification).

Repeat the experiment, using various combinations of filters on a single light, observing:

- the subtractive effect of filtering out more than one selection of spectral colours.

Repeat the experiment, using different filters in two separate lights, observing:

- the additive effect of filtered lights as the reduced spectrum moves towards being put together again.

Scrollers

Remote changing of colour filters by wheels and semaphores, offering a maximum of five alternatives, has been largely superseded by scrollers (Figure 2.34). Selected filters, typically between 2 and 16, are taped together to form a continuous roll driven by a fast motor. Positioning, on the command of a digital signal, is accurate and so fast (scroll time of one second, end to end) that, visually, it is almost instant.

Controls

Lighting pictures are composed by balancing the intensities of selected lighting instruments. These pictures or 'states', and the 'cues' which replace one state by another, are controlled from a desk which is often still referred to as the 'board'. This contraction of 'switchboard' and 'dimmerboard' persists, although operators of today's controls are more concerned with data processing than moving switches or dimmer handles

Figure 2.34 Scroller colour filter
change (Strand Colour Call)

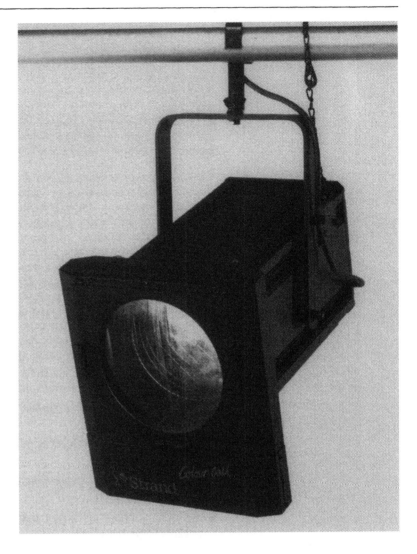

up and down. Intensity control remains the fundamental board function, but
new technologies for colour scrolling and remote instrument focusing are
pointing the way to more comprehensive control facilities.

Dimmers

Today's dimmers, using thyristors, are 'solid-state' with no moving parts.
These dimmers are mounted in portable packs (usually with 3 or 6 dimmers
each), or in permanent racks (usually with multiples of 6 dimmers each, 24
being common) located in the central 'dimmer room' which acts as the
distribution point for feeding all the production lighting sockets around the
theatre. Except in the very smallest installations, the connection between
dimmers and desk is by a single circuit with information passed in
multiplexed form.

Yesterday's dimmers, like steam engines, were exciting to behold.
Today's digital dimmers, although a triumph of self-regulating electronic

wizardry, look like boring cabinets and are one of the few links in the chain that a lighting designer can forget about.

Desks

Every desk provides the basic rehearsal and performance facilities of:

■ access to dimmer channels
■ means of balancing lighting states and recording their content
■ means of recalling these lighting states
■ means of replacing one lighting state by another on cue.

On *manual* boards, access is by miniature levers, scaled from 0° to 100°. With a lever for each dimmer channel, composition of the state of each lighting picture is straightforward. These states are recorded by writing down the percentage level of each dimmer channel lever in each cue. To facilitate recall, there is usually a second set of levers so that the next required state can be prepared (or 'preset') on one set while the current state is held on the other (Figure 2.35). Master faders allow the presets to be crossfaded at any speed, leading or lagging one another if desired.

However, most systems, except the smallest, are based on microprocessors which provide a *memory* capability (Figure 2.36). Access to dimmer channels may still be via a miniature lever per channel, or it may be through other devices of which the numerical keyboard of the pocket calculator is the most common. States are recorded by storing them under

Figure 2.35 Two-preset manual desk (Strand LX)

Figure 2.36 Two-preset manual desk with memory and effects facilities (Strand MX)

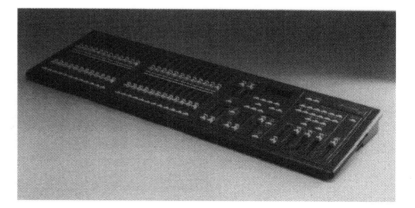

a file number in the system's memory from which they can be recalled for replay via master faders similar to those of a manual system. The essential difference between manual and memory systems is that in the latter there is no need to write down channel levels: memory boards provide instant recording and instant presetting.

While access, record and playback are the essentials, most microprocessor boards have a range of additional features including the use of video screens to display the level of each channel in each memory and the progress of each cue as its programmed time elapses. The possibility of running two sets of cues simultaneously is common, as is the capability to set up chase sequences where a series of channels are programmed to flash on and off in rotation. The ease with which a control system's microprocessor may be programmed allows virtually unlimited scope for complex facilities to be included in the more expensive models (Figures 2.37, 2.38).

Figure 2.37 Compact microprocessor control desk with access to channels and memories by traditional faders or digital keyboard. Upgradable software provides a wide range of operational facilities. (Strand LBX)

Figure 2.38 Advanced microprocessor desk with software options offering sophisticated facilities which can be tailored to the particular requirements of complex productions and large stages. (Strand GeniusPro 530)

All boards have instruction manuals written with varying degrees of clarity and the software often includes help menus which can be displayed on the video screen to take the operator step by step through more complex functions. However, the only real way to find out what a board does is to sit down and play with it.

Experiment with the various operational functions of available boards, observing:

For dimmer response:
■ way in which light intensity varies with the position of the dimmer channel fader as it moves between 0° and 100°
■ delay for filament to warm up when a lamp is faded in from cold.

For channel access:
■ balancing channel faders within a preset
■ call-up of channels by keypad, including 'at' and 'thru' pushes if present
● use of wheel to increase or decrease the level of a selected channel.

For recording:
■ memory file access by dedicated keypad or changing the function of the channel access keypad by a changeover push
■ recording the 'live' lighting state as seen on stage
■ recording a 'blind' lighting state while another state is live on stage
■ recording of fade times, including different times for 'up' (incoming memories) and 'down' (outgoing memories)
■ where system facilities permit, recording of 'profiled' times with accelerations and decelerations rather than regular progress
■ where system facilities permit, recording a move (memorizing only channel levels which change) rather than recording a state (memorizing all channel levels, including those which do not change).

For playback:
■ recalling memory files to the inactive (i.e. presetting) side of the playback faders or pushes
■ selecting automatic sequential recall of memory
■ using 'go to' and 'decimal point' methods (when available) for inserting non-sequential file numbers into the sequential recall facility
■ manual crossfading from one memory to another using master faders, including different rates and leading/lagging of the incoming and outgoing memories
■ automatic crossfading using recording fade times
■ manual intervention of automatic crossfades to speed up or slow down progress.

For effects:
■ by referring to manual or on-screen menu, investigate available effects, including flashing and chasing of channels, groups and memories.

For back-up:
■ provision, if available, for copying recorded files into secondary storage on disk
■ provision for maintaining performance lighting in the event of system failure or part failure.

Projection

The special lighting instruments used for image projection are not unlike profile spotlights with condenser optics. The condenser system is required to provide an even light over the glass slide which is placed at the equivalent position to the gate of a profile spot. Heat resistant glasses and forced fan cooling are necessary to protect the slide at this hottest part of the optical system. The image is focused by an objective lens of appropriate focal length for the size of picture required.

Two types of scene projector are used in theatre: standard 35 mm Kodak carousels and special large format instruments taking 180 mm or even 240 mm slides. To achieve a picture which is bright enough not to appear washed out by contrast with the stage lighting, 35 mm carousel magazine projectors are often adapted to use especially powerful tungsten halogen lamps. The large format projectors use high intensity discharge lamps, dimmed mechanically by motorized glass shutters which are graduated from clear, through increasing greyness, to black. These special projectors and their slides are very expensive indeed and used only on major productions on the biggest stages. Carousels are easier to acquire, and not only are their slides relatively cheap to produce but their slide magazines have a large capacity. The use of 35 mm carousel projectors can become very sophisticated, involving twenty or more projectors controlled by a computer program which advances the slide magazines and crossfades the images.

Experiment with any available projectors, including alternative lenses, observing:

- the 'keystone' distortion when the projected image hits a surface at other than 90°
- images projected on to the front of different types of surface including screens, both white and coloured, and on to painted or textured scenic materials
- images projected on to the rear of different translucent materials including, if available, back projection screen in grey and black plastic
- image quality, including possibility of fine focusing to produce a uniform sharpness of image over the picture area
- image intensity, particularly when spotlighting is focused to miss the screen but illuminate actors standing at various distances from the screen. (Experiment with a black floor and black surround, then introduce increasingly pale-coloured reflective materials into the stage environment.)

Effects

Scene projectors may be used to project moving images and, since very bright pictures are not normally required, 2 kW or 2.5 kW tungsten halogen instruments provide a sufficiently strong image for most stages (Figures 2.39, 2.40). Standard optical effects have images painted or photographed on disks which are motor driven past the condenser lens as an alternative to a fixed slide. Until very recently, speed was changed by varying the position of the drive wheel in a potter's wheel arrangement. So many of these were manufactured that they will doubtless be in use for many years

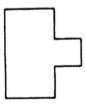

Figure 2.39 International symbol for effects projectors

Figure 2.40 2 kW projector with moving effect and objective lens (Strand Cadenza EP)

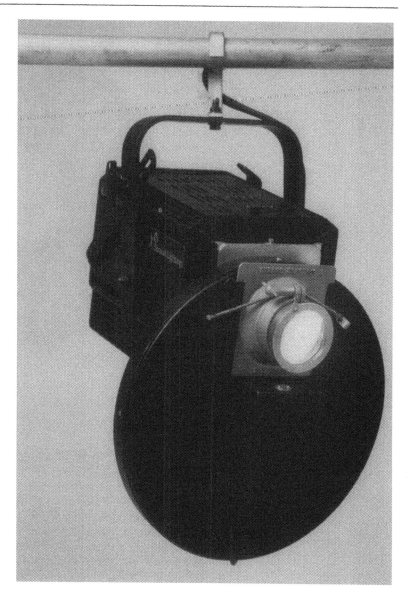

to come. However, the latest models utilize a variable speed motor with the possibility of remote control.

Moving effects projectors can generate realistic pictures of such phenomena as flames, snow, rain and a range of cloud formations produced under various meteorological conditions. Heaving sea waves are projected by motor-driven slides reciprocating up and down rather than rotating. Water ripples can be projected at short range by a ripple box in which a perforated cylinder rotates in front of a long linear lamp. Sometimes the reflected light resulting from such phenomena as fire and water can be more dramatically convincing than a picture of the actual flames or water. This can be achieved by soft focus of pictorial effects, or by profile spots with appropriate gobos and a simple rotating wheel with a series of break-

Figure 2.41 Motorized flicker wheel (Teatro Versa-Disc)

up holes. Alternatively the gobo itself may be given movement. Rotators, with fixed- or variable-speed motors, are available for single or twin gobos. Movement can be clockwise or anticlockwise and the twin types have an option of contrary rotation. A yo-yo model moves two gobos alternately up and down in a reciprocating motion. The quality of the effect is dependent upon careful experiment with speed and focus.

But many effects can be improvised by the simplest means: blue-green filtered light reflected from a tray of water shimmers like light reflected from a river. Changing the filter to red-amber provides shimmering flames, which can also be produced by waving a flag of strips of material in front of a red-amber spotlight.

Strobes emit a rapid series of short flashes which make actor movement appear to be jerky or frozen. Very sophisticated effects can be generated by lasers which can, with the aid of a little smoke, produce three-dimensional images in space.

Experiment with any available effects equipment, observing:
- focus possibilities, including the most realistic picture which may not necessarily be the sharpest image
- result of superimposing the same image from two or more projectors, experimenting with differential focusing to try to give the picture more depth
- movement given to gobo images by motor or manual means
- use of reflected light in which movement is provided either by the light source or by the reflective material.

Rigging

All lighting equipment is designed to operate about the horizontal and vertical axes through the mounting bolt fixed to a hook for use with pipe of scaffolding diameter. Standard rigging arrangements therefore position equipment as follows (Figure 2.42):

■ hanging from a horizontal pipe (known as a bar, except in America) or from a truss
■ bracketed at 90° to a vertical pipe (known as a boom, except in America)
■ placed on a vertical stand by fitting a spigot over the mounting bolt.

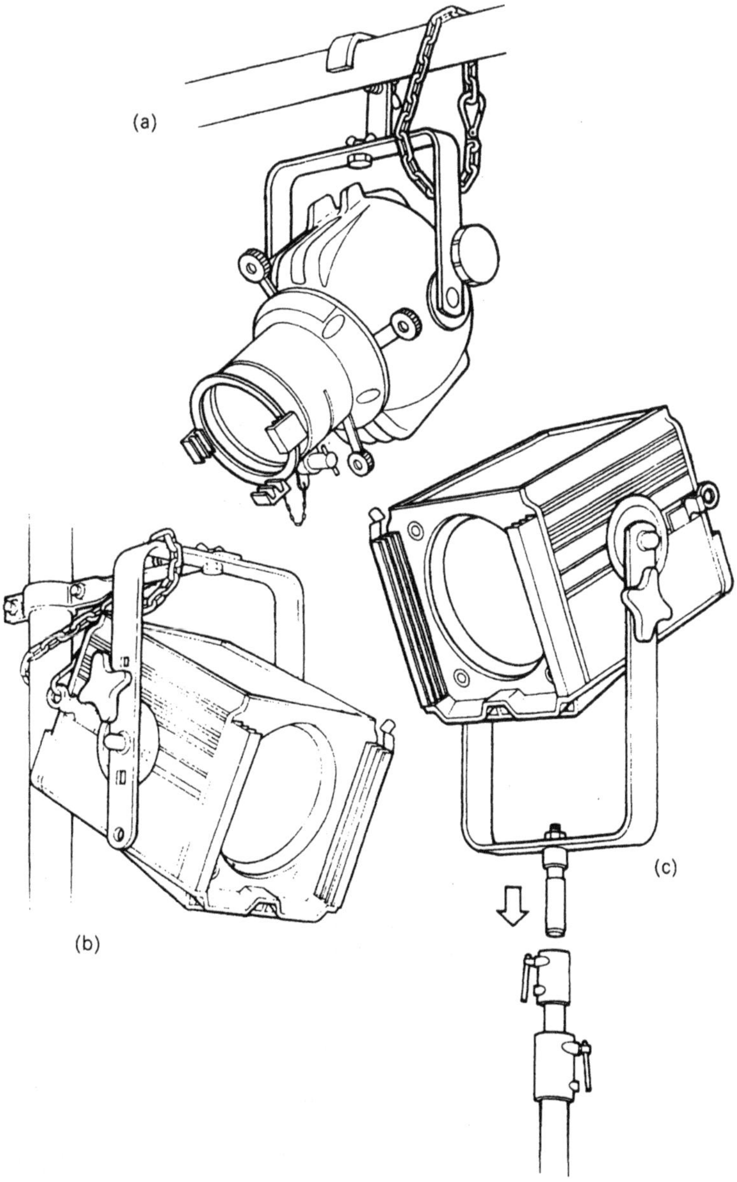

Figure 2.42 Rigging arrangements: (a) hanging on horizontal bar with hook clamp (b) bracketed to vertical boom with boom arm (c) mounted on stand with spigot

(a)

(b)

(c)

3
Lighting safely

A theatre is a potentially dangerous environment. The relative rarity of accidents to audience, actors and technicians is the result not so much of legislation but of continual vigilance based on common sense.

Mechanical

Most lighting accidents are mechanical rather than electrical. Particular attention should be paid to the following points:

- All lights suspended above the stage or auditorium should have safety chains.
- When rigging lights on flying bars, pay scrupulous attention to detail to ensure that all hook clamps are properly tightened, with all accessories such as barndoors and colour frames firmly attached *before* the bar is hoisted.
- When rigging on fixed bars, take special care when carrying lights up ladders, or hoisting them with ropes knotted around their trunnion arms.
- Use ladders, tallescopes and access towers with particular care during focusing, especially on raked floors. Manufacturers' recommendations for use of access equipment, particularly in respect of adjusting outriggers for maximum stability, should be observed without question.
- An adequate crew should be available to steady all ladders, with any movement of wheeled tallescopes and towers always carried out under the direction of the person working at the top of the ladder.
- Tools left at the top of ladders are an obvious source of potential accidents.

Electrical

The cardinal rule is never tamper with, or attempt to modify, any permanent wiring. The power supply to the dimmers and the wiring from the dimmers to the sockets around the theatre must be installed by registered electrical contractors and checked by qualified inspectors on a regular basis. Theatre staff should undertake only temporary rigging, using flexible cable from the socket outlets to the lights. Students undertaking rigging, cabling and focusing should only be permitted to do so under the supervision of experienced stage staff.

When cabling temporary lights from the sockets of a permanent installation, always:

- Ensure that no dimmer is loaded in excess of its rated power. (Most dimmers are rated at 10 amp, making them suitable, at 240 volts, for a maximum load of 2.4 kilowatts (kW); this allows a pair of 1.2 kW spotlights to be fed from one socket. Many installations have a small proportion of 25 amp dimmers and care needs to be taken not to overload standard plugs, sockets and cable when using these circuits).
- Check that there are no cuts or tears in the outer sheathing of cables.
- Check that all cable grips are tight to ensure that no strain is placed on individual wire connections within plugs and sockets. (If any cable grip is loose, open the plug or socket to ensure that the live, neutral and earth wires are tightly attached to their correct terminals.)
- Run cables neatly and securely, without sharp bends, free from strain and, as much as possible, away from heat generated by lights.
- When plugging equipment, assume that the circuit may be live and keep fingers clear of all plug pins.
- When focusing, check that the angle of the light places no strain on the instrument's cable tail.
- Disconnect a spotlight from the supply before opening its lamp house or withdrawing its lamp tray prior to replacing a failed lamp.
- Beware the heat from blown tungsten halogen lamps: they remain dangerously hot for a long time after failing.
- When handling new lamps, use the fresh plastic glove supplied with the lamp in its box.
- Be particularly careful when withdrawing hot gobos from the gates of profile spots.
- Pay scrupulous attention to the licensing authority's regulations governing the use of strobes. Since strobes can trigger epileptic fits in susceptible people, regulations stipulate maximum flash rates and the display of prominent warning notices at entrances to the theatre.

Regular Portable Appliance Testing, known as PAT testing, is mandatory under British law. The tests include polarity, earth connection and insulation. Records must be kept and the most convenient method is to label each item of equipment with its serial number and 'Tested OK – Retest before (date)'. Barcoding the serial number simplifies identification of test history in a computer data storage system.

Operational

Observe blackout discipline at all times:

- Prior to going to blackout at any time other than during performances or rehearsals cued by the stage manager, always shout a clear loud verbal warning.
- When fading up individual dimmer channels for focusing, always bring on the new channel before losing the current one.

4

The lighting process

Lighting any show involves embarking on a voyage of discovery. The surprises which await even the most experienced lighting designer are an inevitable part of any process which involves having ideas and turning these ideas into reality. Even if it were possible to visualize an exact pictorial composition for each moment of the performance, any drama production is in a constant state of inventive development throughout rehearsals. This is particularly intensive during the phase when the actors emerge from the rehearsal room to wear costumes and integrate with all the scenery, lighting and technology of a stage environment. Moreover, the staging of a production is a team effort with the ideas of each member stimulating the whole group. The technical and dress rehearsal phase is a particularly fertile time for this, with the balancing of individual lights to compose pictures not only stimulating the lighting designer's visual thinking but triggering ideas in director, choreographer and scene designer.

This period of working with light is intensively creative but always short. Its success is dependent upon two major factors:

- prior to 'get-in' of the production to the stage: detailed design work to prepare a palette of lights which will meet all foreseeable requirements yet offer scope for responding to the unknown
- during technical dress rehearsals: flexibility by the lighting designer (and the other members of the production team) in responding to the visual stimulation of observing the effect of light on the actors and their scenic environment.

The planning phase of the design provides a chart for the voyage. This planning must ensure the certainty of a 'fail-safe' arrival, while providing scope for an imaginative response to discoveries made in the course of working with light in the context of all the other elements in the production. It must do this within agreed budgets and schedules: the importance of advance planning in ensuring that the maximum proportion of allotted lighting time is available for creative exploration cannot be overemphasized.

The lighting process falls naturally into two phases:

■ work done on text study, thinking, discussing, watching rehearsals, and preparing plans, schedules, etc.; followed by
■ work done on the stage rigging, focusing, plotting, and rehearsing.

Each lighting designer develops their own personal version of the design process. However, there are a number of broad decision areas, with one tending to lead to another in a fairly logical sequence. Self-questioning is central to decision making, with certain standard questions offering a starting point in each decision area.

Initial text study

Every aspect of a stage production stems from the text, and so it is inevitable that the starting point for the preparation of a drama lighting design is a study of the script. The first reading should be quite fast, approaching the text rather like a novel and preferably finishing in one sitting, to get a feel for the play's overall shape, story line and characters. The overall impression gained from this initial read provides a framework for a more detailed analytical study to discover:

■ locations
■ time shifts
■ references to lighting in the dialogue
■ references to lighting in the playwright's stage directions
■ special effects

However, beware (to the point of ignoring) any stage directions which are not the author's but have been added to an acting edition of the script and are probably only relevant to the production they have been taken from.

Initial music study

When music forms an integral part of the work to be performed, study of the text will be followed immediately by immersion in the music score. Indeed, in the case of opera, listening to the music is likely to be simultaneous with, or even to precede, reading the words. For classical ballet or contemporary dance, music has to be the starting point since written material will be restricted to an outline scenario if the work has a story line – or nothing at all if it is an abstract piece.

Few lighting designers can read a music score to the extent of looking at the printed notes and hearing them clearly in their heads. However, people working regularly in dance and opera need to acquire an ability to find their way around a written score, including following the notation while listening to it being played. In recent years, increased availability of recordings, particularly of less frequently staged operas, has made music study easier. Some musicals begin life as commercial recordings and for most a demo tape is made to attract backers and sponsors.

Initial music study normally concentrates upon a broad:

■ familiarization with the musical style
■ response to the atmosphere that it seems to be creating.

Research

Research can help an understanding of some scripts and scores. On second and subsequent readings or listenings, it may be felt that background information in some of the following areas would be helpful:

- historical
- geographical
- sociological
- architectural
- literary (e.g. dramatization of a novel or musical adaptation of a play)
- previous productions.

Establishing the production style

These preliminary script studies prepare the lighting designer for discussion sessions with the rest of the production team. These discussions will evolve the style in which the team propose to approach this particular production of the work. Hopefully, everyone will come to the discussions with a knowledge of the piece together with some ideas about possible ways of staging it. But they will come with an open mind. The director will almost certainly have had the longest preliminary involvement and so, inevitably and appropriately, will have the most developed ideas. Director and set designer will have talked together and so there are very likely to be some sketches and probably a preliminary model. But the lighting designer, wishing to have a positive input into the debate, will be hoping that the set design will not have progressed too far.

At this time, the foremost question in the lighting designer's mind is an all-embracing one:

- What is the role of light going to be in this production?

The search for an answer leads to a consideration of such topics as:

- How naturalistic?
- How selective?
- How atmospheric?
- How softly diffuse?
- How sculptural?
- How coloured?
- Any projection?
- Any special effects?

Such questions, if asked directly, tend to be conversation stoppers. The lighting designer has to tease the answers out gently. It is rarely easy because we can never be sure that two people are imagining the same pictures when agreeing about words. For example, when the director or the set designer talk about 'dark', are we sure whether they mean low intensity or deeply saturated colour? Only careful cross-questioning will confirm.

As consensus begins to emerge on an approach to the production in general and its lighting in particular, the lighting designer considers whether any details of the scenery model conflict with the proposed use of light. This includes such points as:

● Is everyone fully aware that the dramatic directional light obtained on the model by shining an anglepoise desk light from upstage left will tend to be diluted by essential frontal light for the actors' faces?
● How reflective is the floor? Is everyone fully aware that, while a glossy floor can look wonderful and provide faces with a flatteringly soft uplight from below, reflections from even a single beam can spoil the intended dramatic effect of picking an actor out from surrounding darkness?
● Are there any surfaces of the set which are likely to collect so much light that they should be painted or stained to a considerably darker shade in order to appear on the stage as they do on the model?
● Are there any possible minor modifications to the set which would be acceptable to its designer and improve access for light from desirable angles?
● Is there likely to be any difficulty in lighting faces because large areas of scenery are coloured in tones similar to flesh?
● Is there likely to be any conflict between the filters that are appropriate for the costumes and those for the scenery?

Analysing the production

Once the production is in rehearsal, the lighting designer observes how the intended use of the set develops as the director works with the actors. This will lead to analysing the use of the set in terms of the agreed lighting styles. Self-questioning will include:

● How does the stage divide into areas which require independent selection by light?
● Does the size of these areas necessitate further subdivision for practical reasons?
● How does the stage divide by colour?
● How many different colours are required for mixing in each of these divisions?
● Does the colour division correspond to the area division?
● Which lights are so critical in the size, shape and colour of their beams as to require specially focused instruments (rather than equipment that doubles as general purpose acting area lights)?
● Are there any special effects?

Instrument location

Once a breakdown has been established of where there should be light and where there is a need to mix colours, consideration of the direction of the light leads naturally to decision about where instruments should be positioned. These decisions are based on ideals which then have to be compromised by practicalities, particularly auditorium architecture and scenery positions. Consequently, the initial question is:

● Where are the *ideal* instrument positions for lighting each acting area and for lighting selected elements of scenery?

These positions will be those that allow the light to strike actors or scenery at appropriate angles to provide the desired mix of visibility, sculpting, selectivity and shadow. These angles are determined mainly by experience derived from observation of cause and effect in the kind of situations discussed in Chapter 1 and developed in the practical exercises in Part Two of this book.

Once ideal positions have been determined, practical compromise is reached by a further question sequence:

- Where are the nearest available existing positions?
- Are there instruments in this position as part of the theatre's permanent or normal rig?
- If any of the existing positions impose an unacceptable degree of compromise, is there any possibility of a temporary rigging solution?

Instrument selection

When positions have been decided, the instrument type for each position may be selected. Ideals are again the starting point:

- What is the *ideal* type of instrument for each of the chosen positions?

Choice will be based mainly on the quality of light desired and the amount of control required over beam size and shape, as discovered from the type of observations suggested in Chapter 2. This choice will also take into consideration the relative time required to focus simpler and more complex instruments.

Instrument choice often requires less compromise than other decision areas. Nevertheless, it usually has to be subjected to another self-questioning sequence:

- How far does the available equipment match this ideal requirement?
- Are there instruments of the right type already in some of the positions as part of the theatre's current rig?
- If some of the instruments already in position are not exactly ideal, are they sufficiently close for an acceptable compromise?
- After determining priorities, can available equipment be matched to requirement in order to minimize rental?
- After allocating as much available equipment as possible, is the remaining requirement within the rental budget?
- If it is over budget, can we compromise further?
- Or can we make a sufficiently strong case for a contingency allocation?

Selecting filters

The role of colour in the production having been determined as part of the decisions about lighting style, an appropriate filter has to be allocated for each instrument. While a wide range of filters may be used on scenery, the colour for most of the acting areas in a particular production tends to be based on a relatively small group of filters selected for that production. Choice is narrowed down in two steps arising mainly from style decisions:

■ hue: basic spectrum division into red, yellow, orange, blue, etc.
■ saturation: range of dilution from paler to deeper.

These are followed by two steps arising mainly from the pigments used in the scenery, costumes and make-up:

■ tendency: blues with highish red or green contents, ambers with varying proportions of orange and yellow
■ filter: the actual numbered filter from a particular manufacturer's range.

Decisions in these final two steps are likely to involve experiment with filter samples, a light source, the scenic model and costume fabric swatches.

Priorities

Lighting designers devote a lot of their lives to consideration of priorities. At each phase of the design process, first assessment of the requirement usually seems irreconcilable with budgeted finance or scheduled time. However, continual examination and re-examination to determine priorities enable the apparently minimum number of areas, colours and instruments to be reduced even further. Determining priorities is hard and time-consuming work, but finding an optimum which is closer to minimum than to maximum usually results in lighting which benefits from being simpler, cleaner and bolder. Self-questioning is along the following lines:

● Do we really need four separately controlled areas in this part of the stage? Perhaps we could amalgamate two of them?
● Do we really need to have a double-colour cover in all these areas? Perhaps one or two could be basically neutral with some simple colour toning?
● Do we really need to light all the areas from so many angles? Perhaps some of the areas are used sufficiently less to be given a simpler treatment?
● How vital is each special? Does its use, perhaps for only thirty seconds, justify the removal of an instrument from an evening of general use?
● Could we squash an existing Fresnel's barndoors rather than shutter and soften a rented profile?
● Could diffused PCs substitute for some Fresnels?
● Would diffusing and stretching with silk filters enable us to use these surplus parcans?
● Are all filter requirements absolutely precise or could some near equivalents from stock be substituted?

Documenting the design

The major document of a lighting design is a scale plan showing:

■ location of each instrument
■ precise type of instrument including beam angle and lamp power (stencil outlines are used to convey as much as possible of this information (Figures 4.1, 4.2))

Figure 4.1 Stencil with international symbols for family types of lighting instruments (ADB)

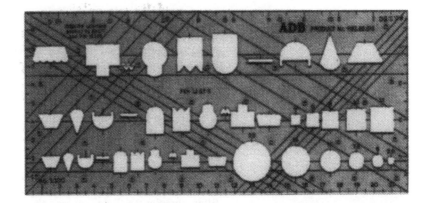

Figure 4.2 Stencil with symbols for specific models of lighting instruments (Strand)

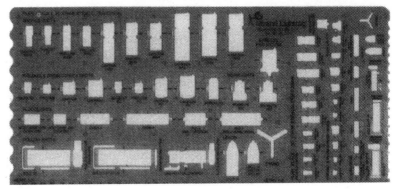

- accessories such as barndoors, gobos and irises
- filter numbers
- control channel numbers
- abbreviated indications of focus direction.

This lighting plan is supported by a series of schedules listing:

- detailed focus information for each instrument
- patching schedule (if channel control numbers differ from dimmer socket numbers)
- all instruments and accessories
- all rigging equipment including cabling
- equipment on rental
- 'colour call' showing number of pieces required of each size of each filter.

Although most plans still originate on a drawing board (Figure 4.3), with their supporting schedules written or typed, there is an accelerating move towards using computers. Several proprietary software programs, including Laplight, Lightwright and Express-Track, produce every conceivable piece of lighting paperwork on all standard types of personal computer. Their capability includes tracking sheets to record the level of every channel in every cue. Programs such as Modelbox Autolight allow lighting plans to be drawn on a computer video screen, and the software generates all necessary schedules when requested by a few simple keystrokes (Figure 4.4).

Figure 4.3 Part of a lighting plan
drawn with stencils

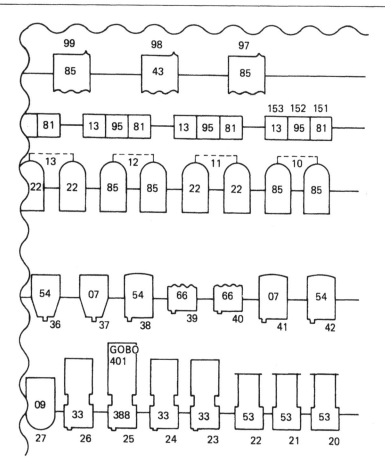

Figure 4.3 Part of a lighting plan drawn with stencils

Documentation for a production, drawn up by the technical director or production manager, should include a section on the centreline showing the heights of all masking, lights, rostra and hanging scenery. Any flying pieces should be shown at both their in and out positions ('deads' in the UK, 'trims' in the US).

The final, but indispensable, document is the 'cue synopsis', which should be developed by the lighting designer during run-throughs in the rehearsal room and agreed with director, choreographer, set designer and the member of the stage management team who will be calling the cues. A cue synopsis should list:

- cue number
- up and down timings in seconds for incoming and outgoing memories
- position in script
- cue intent – a brief description of what is intended to happen.

Communicating design intentions

Scenery, costume and prop designs are small scale models or drawings of what will actually appear on the stage. The graphics of a lighting design, however, bear no pictorial relation to the stage lighting intentions which

Figure 4.4 Part of lighting plan
drawn with computer graphics
(Modelbox Autolight)

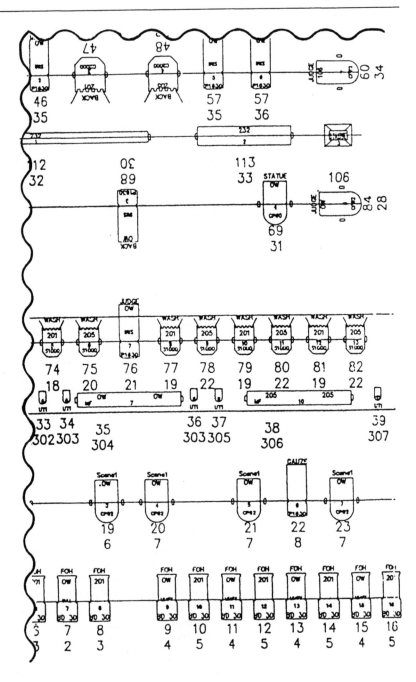

they convey. Moreover, the main purpose of the lighting designer's work
up to this point is to assemble an appropriate palette to paint the actors and
their scenic environment when they are brought together on the stage.
Consequently, at the point when a production moves out of the rehearsal
room on to the stage, less is known of the lighting designer's intentions
than of any other member of the team. However, although the visual
aspects of the lighting are unrealized visions which exist only in an

exchange of visually inadequate words, it is vital that the *technical* intentions are communicated to the right people.

The plan which was the lighting designer's principal work surface during the key decision phases of the design process, now becomes the major communication document. It carries all the essential information required by the electrics crew for rigging. It also gives the set designer, stage management, stage crew and flymen a clear confirmation of the space allocated to all lighting bars, booms, ladders and stands.

Once the plan copies have been distributed and recipients have had an opportunity to examine them, the lighting designer should ask about problems rather than wait to be told. And, of course, any subsequent changes should be notified to anyone likely to be affected, even in the most minor way.

Equipment preparation

Once the plans and schedules are complete, all that remains to be done before moving the production from rehearsal room to stage is to ensure that the equipment has been prepared as far as possible. The following points should be noted:

- All good rental companies maintain and test their equipment to a standard whereby, although not necessarily looking like new, it performs as new. Renting from cheaper companies who operate to a lower standard than this can turn out to be an expensive decision.
- Lights owned by the theatre or the production company should be checked for cleanliness and mechanical operation (especially shutters, lenses and tilt-locks). Although this may only be feasible with equipment which is out of use during the preparation period, it is equipment not currently in use that is most likely to be dirty or faulty.
- Accessories (gobos, irises, barndoors, safety chains, etc.), rigging (bars, hook clamps, booms, boom arms etc.), cables, plugs and sockets should be counted and examined.
- Filters should be cut to size, framed and labelled.
- All preparations should be made on the principle of assuming the worst: check, check and recheck.

Rigging

The major purpose of all the design work carried out prior to the move from rehearsal room to theatre is to ensure that all stage time available for lighting can be used to maximum advantage. On stage, the key creative phases in the process are focusing and plotting. But before they can be started, all lights have to be rigged and scenery positioned.

Fast, safe and efficient rigging is a management exercise involving coordination both within the electrics crew and between the electrics and other departments. It is particularly important to integrate scenery hanging and light hanging. Start, for example, with lights downstage and scenery upstage, then change over; follow by electrics keeping clear of the acting area (rigging booms and front of house (FOH)) while the stage crew build the set; etc., etc. Attention to the following points during rigging will help to prepare for focusing:

- Before carrying any spotlight up a ladder or flying it out on a bar, check that all shutters are out, any gobo and/or filter is in position and the safety chain is fitted.
- To eliminate time-consuming trial and error when plugging up, ensure that all plugs on a multicore or harness of individual cables are numbered.
- Check the slack of each instrument's cable tail, and possible obstruction from adjacent instruments, to ensure that each light has freedom to point at its intended target.
- Prior to starting to focus, flash out the complete rig to ensure that each light is working and connected to its assigned channel.

Focusing

Although detailed design work results in each light having an allotted function, the actual focusing process is a time of intense creativity. It is a time when lighting designers must remain flexible, ready to react to any unforeseen opportunity, yet aware of possible knock-on consequences of radical changes to the plan. Nevertheless, the way that a light beam accidentally strikes a piece of scenery when the instrument is first switched on, possibly even when flashed as part of a rigging check, may trigger an idea in the mind of the lighting designer or any other member of the team who happens to be watching. Lighting designers do need to cultivate open but disciplined minds!

The tried and tested way of focusing is for the lighting designer to stand in the centre of the beam with back to the light, giving instructions by word and gesture to the electrician up the ladder. This enables a check of actor light, by watching shadow rather than being dazzled, while noting the effect of the beam, especially its edge, on scenery. Ideally the only instrument alight should be the one currently being focused – unless when checking the overlapping join between lights for adjacent areas. Attention to the following points should help to reduce the likelihood of a refocus:

- Actor definitely lit within all expected parts of the beam.
- Centre of light beam at face level, taking particular care to keep PC and Fresnel beams high prior to barndooring.
- Adjacent areas comfortably overlapping, both left/right and upstage/downstage.
- Beam edges soft (unless hardened for a definite purpose) and, whenever possible, lost by coinciding with a feature of the set's structure or decoration.

The whole process is quicker and easier when the lighting designer, projecting with a loud clear voice, gives simple instructions worded in terms of available adjustments like up/down, left/right, bigger/smaller, harder/softer, shutter the top in, etc., accompanying the words with simple gestures like finger pointing to emphasize direction and hand waving to indicate shutters.

Plotting

Lighting states for each cue are composed at a session usually referred to as 'plotting'. The alternative Canadian term 'level setting' captures the essence of what actually happens: deciding which channels are alight and their intensity levels. Actors are not present at a traditional plotting rehearsal: 'walkers', often junior members of the stage management team, take up positions in the acting areas as required. When control was by the old manual boards without memory facilities, and alterations at subsequent rehearsals were difficult, the balancing of levels had to be particularly accurate. With today's memory boards, the overall picture can be composed but the fine balancing of the acting areas left until later rehearsals with the actors. The presence of actors is particularly important in modern dance where there is frequently no scenery and the dancers both define the space and populate it. Some points relevant to plotting:

- The key piece of equipment is the lighting designer's eye.
- The lighting designer's eye is supported by the eyes of director, choreographer, set and costume designers – all of whom have different visual priorities. Hopefully, the lighting designer will be able to produce a result which incorporates all these specialist priorities. However, some compromise is inevitable from time to time.
- There is considerable merit in the old saying: 'When in doubt, up a point'. If the production team who know every detail of the production are in any doubt, it is very likely that the audience will experience visibility problems.
- Some lighting designers use point 7 (i.e. 70%) as their initial maximum level: this leaves scope for both increases and decreases during subsequent balancing. (The author often starts plotting sessions by saying to the board operator: 'When I ask for a channel number, bring it to 7 unless I give you a level.')
- Many lighting designers find channel numbers easier to locate on a small simplified 'magic sheet' than on a copy of the full 1:25 lighting plan.

Technical rehearsing

The 'tech' is the rehearsal when the actors are coordinated with scenery, costumes, lighting and all the technology of a stage environment. Only the orchestral players are likely to be missing, although the conductor and a pianist will be in the pit. Most technical rehearsals, inevitably, are long and slow, stopping for each and every problem to be solved and each uncertainty to be clarified. For lighting, the key areas for attention and possible modification are:

- positions of cues
- timings of cues
- balance within cue states.

Positions and timings are interlinked: if a cue does not seem to be working, the answer may be to speed it up or slow it down, perhaps with a changed differential between up and down speeds; or it may be to give the 'go' sooner or later; or possibly a mixture of both. Fine balance, particularly between the relative light intensity on several actors, can only really be achieved when they are all in position. This balancing takes place during the technical rehearsals and is likely to continue during subsequent dress rehearsals until the first performance.

Dress rehearsing

Whereas the actors concentrated on mechanics at the technical rehearsal, dress rehearsals are a time for acting. In quiet periods between cues, it may be possible for the lighting designer to adjust intensities, but nothing must be done which disturbs the flow of the performance or upsets the concentration of actors, board operator or stage manager. This is mostly a time for viewing the stage from different angles and making notes for adjustments to be made after the rehearsal. But beware of making too many adjustments: there comes a point when the apparent solution can cause more problems than it cures!

Performing

On the first night, there is nothing left for the lighting designer to do except try to enjoy the performance and, if necessary, take notes. (The lighting designer may, of course, also be the board operator, but this is only feasible if the desk is sufficiently portable to be placed in the auditorium alongside the production desk during rehearsals when it is essential that the lighting designer remains in close contact with the rest of the production team, sharing their view of the stage.) The lighting designer, or an assistant, should keep an eye on the production from time to time during the early days of the run: performances mature and this can involve some minor repositioning of actors. Electrics crews normally carry out a daily lamp check, using a memory which includes all instruments at a low intensity level, to discover whether any blown lamps need replacing. They also have regular focus checks, paying particular attention to instruments which are likely to be knocked by scenic movements.

5

Analysing lighting

Response to designed light, like response to any art, involves subjective judgements in which the final arbiter can only be the reaction of an eye which feels either that the light looks right or that it does not. Lighting designers need to develop confidence in the response of their eyes but, because theatre is a group activity, they must remain sensitive to the opinions of the rest of the production team. And, no matter how sensitive a lighting designer's eye, the opinion of other eyes can be very important because, under pressure, the lighting designer may be concentrating so much on detail as to misjudge the total effect.

But just how do we begin to decide whether the light for a production is any good or not? What do we look for and how do we analyse our response? Whether that response be subjective or objective, it is helped by being broken down into a series of small steps. These can form the basis of group discussion although their major use is likely to be for self-questioning.

There are two basic situations, depending on whether or not we have been personally involved in staging the production.

Non-involved analysis

When lighting people spend an evening at a theatre, particularly if they are students or designers in the early years of their careers, it is inevitable that they concentrate a disproportionate amount of their attention upon the light. Indeed they are probably the only people in the theatre who are consciously aware of the light. This is necessary if they are to analyse it, but they must train themselves to respond to the whole show. It is possible, but takes years of practice, for a lighting designer to relax at a performance and enjoy it, noticing the lighting only when it distracts. But most light-aware people will find themselves responding by analysing along the following lines:

- Did the light fully support the production?
- Was the light fully integrated – and consistent in its style? Were its priorities right – and its colours?

- Did we always see the actors as clearly as we would have wished? And were they sufficiently well sculpted?
- Was the scenery enhanced by the light? Was it well sculpted – or flattened? Were its mechanics disguised – or exposed?
- Was the light too naturalistic? Or should it have been more naturalistic?
- Could the light have contributed more to the atmosphere?
- Should the acting areas have been more tightly selected?
- If automated spotlights were used, did they make a contribution that would have been difficult, or even impossible, with conventional equipment?

Not knowing any of the background to the production, one might look around to consider:

- How good do the FOH lighting positions appear to be?
- Do the scenery and masking seem to be blocking off potentially useful lighting positions?

and speculate on:

- How close does this final result resemble what the production team set out to achieve?
- Are there indications of compromise? If so, do we suspect lack of equipment, or perhaps too much equipment, or insufficient time?
- If we had been the lighting designer, would we have wished to do differently?
- If so, would our design have integrated with the rest of the production? Or would we have wished to alter that also?

Involved analysis

It is inevitable that any response during rehearsals is very subjective. However, after a run of performances the response becomes more objective and, on returning after a break of a few days, it is possible to view with an eye which, although it can never be fresh, can certainly be fresher. The analysis is basically similar to that above but is more detailed, has no need for speculation and considers lighting management in addition to lighting design:

- Did the light support the production as fully as we hoped?
- How close did the final result match what we set out to achieve?
- Were we flexible in responding to changing ideas as rehearsals developed – and in adapting our plans accordingly?
- Did the palette of focused lights provide everything the production team hoped for?
- Were we flexible in developing ideas, where appropriate, or did we stick too rigidly to the original concept?
- Was there more compromise than anticipated, perhaps because of shortage of equipment, or lack of time?
- If there was a lack of time, did this result from insufficient allocated lighting time, or was time reduced as a knock-on consequence of problems in other areas? Did any insufficiency in the allocated time result from trying to use too much equipment? Was any time wasted by poorly maintained equipment?

- Were any problems caused by poor FOH lighting positions? And did we make the best use of the available FOH positions?
- Did scenery and masking block off any useful lighting positions?
- Did we make the best use of available on-stage positions?
- Was each instrument in the rig able to do its planned job? Or did scenery or masking ever get in the way? If the latter, should our planning have been able to anticipate?
- If automated spotlights were used, did they contribute positively to lighting quality and/or lighting management?
- If automated spotlights had been available, might they have made a contribution to lighting quality and/or lighting management?
- Was the lighting style appropriate – and consistent? Was it fully integrated? Were its priorities right?
- Was the light too naturalistic? Or should it have been more naturalistic?
- Could the light have contributed more to the atmosphere?
- Was the choice of colour filters atmospherically supportive? And did they enhance the scenery and costumes?
- Was the scenery generally enhanced by the light? Was it well sculpted – or flattened? Were its mechanics disguised – or exposed?
- Should the acting areas have been more tightly selected?
- Did we always see the actors as clearly as we would have wished? And were they sufficiently well sculpted?
- Given a second chance, what would we do differently? Would we change the concept – or its practical implementation?

Project analysis

Each of the projects in Part Two of this book includes a version of the analysis which focuses on the questions which are particularly appropriate to the objectives of that project. It is intended that these analyses should form the basis of an agenda for group discussion at the conclusion of each project.

This discussion should also include consideration of the efficiency of individual and group lighting management in carrying out the project. For this a common agenda is proposed, including assessment of time organization, equipment handling and communications. Perhaps the most central of all is communications – for theatre is primarily a people industry.

Part Two
Projects

Introduction to the projects

The aim of these projects is to develop an understanding of both lighting design and lighting management by placing students in situations where they can discover how to use light on the stage. By limiting the number of variables, each project concentrates attention on specific problems. The starting point is the cornerstone of all lighting design: a study of the consequences of the angle at which light hits objects and actors. From this, the project sequence is structured so that one discovery leads to another, with each project placing increasing demands upon the contribution of light.

Most of the projects include a proportion of lights with type and hanging position specified. This is mainly to minimize the time spent in changing the rig between each designer. However, it also reduces the number of variables and represents the real situation in many theatres.

The plans show the projects set in a simple rectangular studio space with no permanent installation other than a simple overall scaffolding-pipe grid (Figure P.1). However, the projects may be adapted for most available spaces including proscenium stages with sophisticated equipment. The minimum viable height of the grid is about 4.5 m or 14 ft. It is quite possible to work with a lower grid, but shifting a light only a few centimetres along a bar on a low grid has such a major effect on angle as to make unnecessary difficulties for inexperienced students – to the extent of obscuring basic principles. The grids have been drawn with the minimum number of bars. Many installations have more, and experienced students should also have the option of inserting short additional bars if they can argue the case for wishing to make the experiment.

International symbols have been used to indicate instrument types. Although many PC focus spots have been indicated, the Fresnels found in most older installations may be substituted.

Most projects end with a note on the possible use of automated lights. This technology is unlikely to be available in most lighting discovery laboratories – at least for the next few years. However, after carrying a project through with conventional equipment, it is interesting to speculate on the contribution that automated lights might make. To stimulate debate, the notes are in question form. It must be emphasized that, in situations where these 'moving lights' are available, it is advisable to tackle the project initially with conventional fixed equipment.

Figure P.1 (a) Basic studio grid plan (b) section through studio width (c) section through studio length

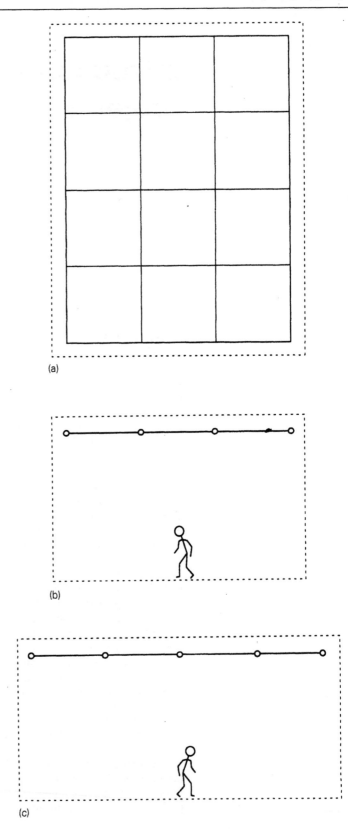

(a)

(b)

(c)

Scenic environments are simple, with many of the earlier projects requiring only table and chairs. Where a more elaborate setting is indicated, this can be devised from very basic rostra and step units – with opportunities for imaginative use of found objects. Black masking has been drawn in appropriate positions to define the limits of the stage space. Soft black legs at the sides and tracked tabs at the rear are the simplest to use. If possible, these should be the straight blacks which have now largely replaced traditional full blacks in standard stage practice. However, black masking flats may, of course, be used if more convenient. Borders have not been indicated but should be introduced for some projects if carried out on a stage with suspension lines allowing easy deading.

Each project comprises:

- statement of the project's primary objectives
- suggested equipment rig, with notes on possible variations to enable adjustment for available equipment and space, plus indicators for directions of possible further exploration as work on the project develops
- synopsis of lighting cue (Q) requirements with notes, where appropriate, of the kind that might be provided by members of the production team
- brief analysis of the problems likely to be encountered in the project, with emphasis on possible conflicts between the various objectives.

As far as possible, the projects should be carried out in accordance with the reality of normal theatre procedures as outlined in Chapter 4. It is particularly important that every member of a group should make a design commitment on paper before the practical exploration starts.

Projects should be carried out under the guidance of a tutor, who need not necessarily be an experienced lighting designer but should have wide ranging production experience and an eye for the possibilities of visual theatre. It is, of course, important that technical support is available to ensure that equipment is used and maintained in a safe manner.

The most difficult part of the tutor's role is deciding when to offer a comment or remain silent. Comments can be more effective when offered as questions – 'Do you feel that the light on the girl is a bit toppy or is the steep angle justified by the short shadow?' – and used principally to maintain impetus or to veer the work in a more positive direction. In some situations, the tutor may act as director, answering questions to supplement information given in the brief. At other times, it may be appropriate for student lighting designers to act as their own directors, supplying their own answers with tutorial help in considering the alternatives.

The optimum size of group to tackle a project is the number required to keep everyone occupied with tasks. These tasks are rotated to offer all participants an opportunity to undertake the key jobs of designing, handling the lights during focusing and operating the board. By including short spells of observation in the rota, the size of the group can be expanded a little. Observers should be encouraged to discuss what they see, with the tutor adopting an *animateur* role in stimulating discussion.

The normal roles for rotation within a group are:

- lighting designer
- crew chief (who organizes personnel and technical matters in order to leave the designer free to concentrate on lighting)
- focuser (up the ladder)
- ladder crew (moving and holding ladders)
- filter crew (locating, cutting and framing filters, as appropriate)

- board operator
- observers.

The suggested sequence is:

- Determine any modifications required to adapt the project to the venue and available equipment.
- Schedule a deadline for completion of plans and allocate slots for implementing each design and discussing the results.
- Hold a briefing to ensure that everyone understands the project, including maximum stage time allocated for each design.
- Each student prepares a lighting design consisting of a plan plus appropriate supporting documentation.
- Each student presents his or her design to the group, explaining intentions and answering questions.
- The tutor chooses the first design for implementation. This is neither the potentially best nor worst, but is the one that, initially, seems likely to throw up the most interesting points. (Whether subsequent designs are chosen at this time is optional. If a design requires a lot of filter organization, there is much to commend having the next one in preparation, particularly if spare hands are available. However, it is useful to have the option of moving on to whichever design seems to lead on from problems which have just been exposed.)
- Optional additional instruments for the first design are rigged.
- The designer supervises focus followed by plotting of cues, as per standard professional procedures.
- The cue sequence is run through with members of the group taking the acting roles. (Repeat to give everyone an opportunity of seeing.)
- The discussion, chaired by the tutor, starts with the lighting designers being invited to comment on their own work. Then all members of the group are encouraged to voice opinions and ask questions. The light should always be set to the cue state under discussion. Project material includes an analysis agenda, tailored to each particular project.
- After the experience of seeing early designs implemented and discussed, later students should be given the opportunity to modify their plans if they wish.

For some projects, particularly 10, 12, 13, 16 and 17, design work at the drawing board should lead to a palette of lighting possibilities which allows for a considerable degree of experimental composition during the practical phase. In these cases it may be appropriate for limited facilities to be made available for experiments with light during the planning phase of the design.

For some projects and with some student groups, it may be appropriate to divide the drawing board phase of the design process into sections with target dates for completion of each phase, for example:

- Initial thoughts on form of setting and how it will respond under light.
- Setting ideas established and cue synopsis under way (perhaps with story board).
- Setting designed and draft synopsis complete.
- Lighting positions chosen.
- Lighting instruments chosen.
- Colour decisions started.
- Plans complete.

Project 1
Objects and actors

This project may be used as a very first introduction to lighting actors and their stage environment. However, since it explores such fundamentals, it is also of value to students who already have acquired some basic understanding of light.

Objectives

To explore the effect of light from different angles on (a) objects and (b) actors; to explore the interaction between light for actors and light for their stage environment.

Setting

If possible the exercise should be set within a neutral surround of black masking as indicated on the plan (Figure P.2). The scenic object should be a simple three-dimensional piece with scope for modelling: a half-rounded column is ideal (Figure P.3).

Rig

A grid of 18 spotlights provides a series of alternative lighting angles. Two additional spotlights on movable stands are available for lower angles.

The spots are simple focus PCs or Fresnels. Barndoors should not be provided initially, but only made available if and when their necessity has been established.

Substitution of profile spots should certainly only be permitted if the requirement is definitely proved and only once the progress of the exercise is considerably advanced.

The exercise should be carried out in 'open white' without colour filters. Diffuser filters should only be allowed after students have demonstrated a full understanding of the standard focus adjustments on the spotlights.

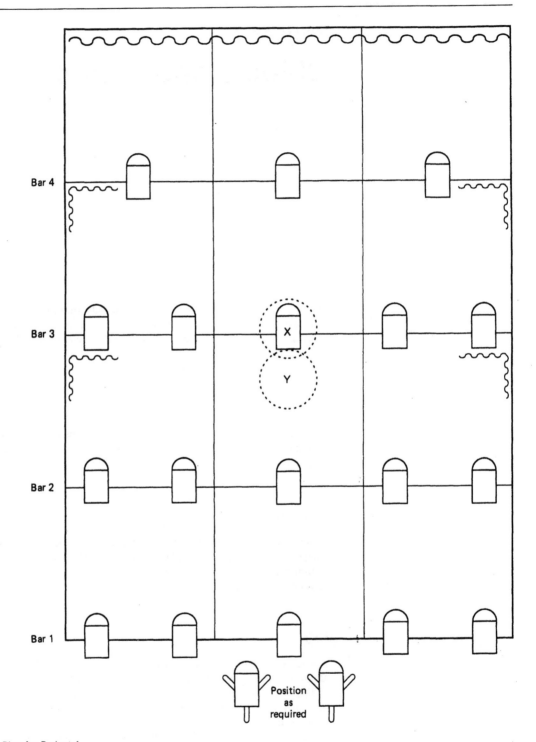

Figure P.2 Plan for Project 1

Figure P.3 Any type of pillar makes a good scenic object for this project. It could be (a) Doric or (b) Ionic, although it need not necessarily have any kind of ornamentation. The important factor is that it should present a three-dimensional curved surface to the audience: the simplest construction is half round (i.e. 180°)

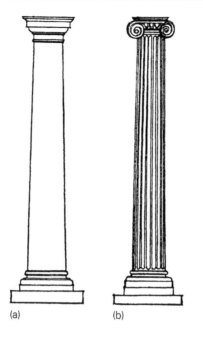

(a)   (b)

Contraction and expansion

The number of lights indicated is the ideal. If this has to be reduced due to lack of equipment, remove in the following order until down to number available: 2 and 4 on bar 1; 2 and 4 on bar 2; 1 and 3 on bar 4; 2 and 4 on bar 3. Rig expansion should only be contemplated after exploring all possibilities of the basic rig: extra equipment can then be added to provide any additional angles that experiment has shown to be worth trying.

Synopsis

Q1. Light a column (or alternative object) in position X (i.e. under centre light on bar 3).
Q2. With the column removed, light an actor in position X.
Q3. With the column replaced in position X, light an actor in position Y.

Possible problems

■ Experiment should demonstrate that there are various methods of lighting the column to enhance its sculptural quality. Some of these methods will indicate the direction of the light.
■ Since the column does not have a face with eyes and teeth, most of the options that worked for the column are unlikely to prove satisfactory for lighting the actor.
■ Further experiment should demonstrate alternative solutions which offer both visibility and modelling, perhaps with a feeling of direction. However, some conflict between good visibility and good modelling can

be expected, with differences of opinion between individual members of the group about the optimum balance.

■ If different lighting is found to be desirable for column and actor, some conflict of priorities seems inevitable when the actor is placed immediately in front of the column.

Analysis of results

● Was there more need for compromise than anticipated?
● Were we able to keep the scene isolated with no light hitting the masking? Better still, were we able to keep a small amount of unlit floor between the light beams and the masking?
● Should the area have been more tightly selected?
● Was the column generally enhanced by the light, sculpted rather than flattened?
● Did we always see the actor as clearly as we would have wished?
● And was the actor sufficiently well sculpted?
● Another time, what would we do differently?

Assessment of lighting management

● Organization of time?
● Communications?
● Equipment handling?

Project 2
Covering smoothly

Objective

To provide an even sculptural illumination for an acting area.

Setting

A neutral surround of black masking is desirable (Figure P.4).

Rig

A grid of 15 spotlights is arranged in a slightly different configuration to that of Project 1. The project should commence with simple PC or Fresnel spots fitted with barndoors. Once the problem has been solved, or at least is on the way to being solved, profiles may (and should) be substituted.

Contraction and expansion

Expansion of the rig is not recommended for this project, but if the number of lights has to be reduced because of lack of equipment, this may be done by removing 2 and 5 from bar 3, then 1 and 3 from bar 4.

Cue synopsis

Q1. Light actors in the area indicated by the broken line.
Q2. Tighten to the area indicated by the dotted line.

Possible problems

- Remember that the broken and dotted lines indicate areas where actors can walk and their faces will be lit: this is not the same as areas of lit

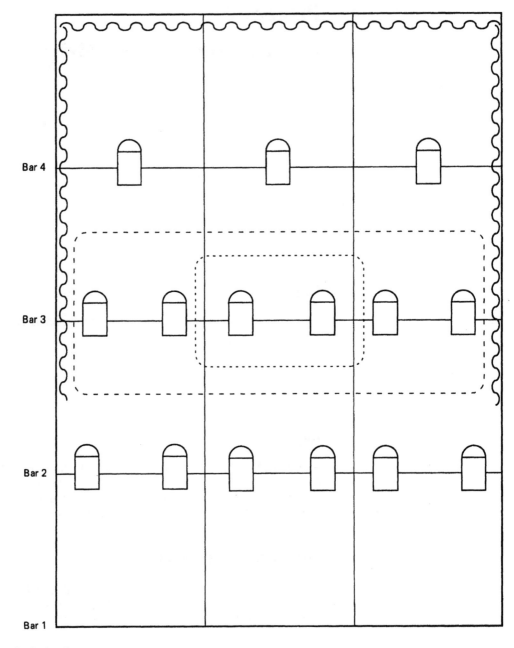

Figure P.4 Plan for Project 2

stage floor. Face areas and floor areas cannot be identical but we should try to relate them as closely as is practical.

■ There is an inevitable conflict between sculptural modelling and visibility: achieving a visually satisfying compromise is a major component of lighting design.

Analysis of results

- Did we always see the actors as clearly as we would have wished?
- And were they sufficiently well modelled?
- Did we achieve the optimum compromise between visibility and modelling?
- Were we able to keep the scene isolated, minimizing light spill on to the masking?
- Did we achieve the closest possible relation between face areas and floor areas?
- Another time, what would we do differently?

Assessment of lighting management

- Organization of time?
- Communications?
- Equipment handling?

If automated lights available

Could the area be tightened by remote focusing in conjunction with pan and tilt?

Project 3
Selecting space

Objectives

To explore the use of light for (a) defining space and (b) concentrating audience attention on selected areas within that space.

Setting

Plain scenic flats indicate the entrance to a small room with a table and two chairs (Figure P.5). A black masking surround is desirable.

Rig

The lighting grid provides 6 profile and 6 focus (PC or Fresnel) spots. Additional lights, up to a maximum of 6, may be hung at any chosen positions on the grid.

Contraction and expansion

If equipment is scarce, remove in the sequence of 2 and 5 from the profile spot bar followed by 2 and 5 from the focus spot bar, and then reduce the number of permitted additionals. Expansion of this exercise by making extra instruments available is advised only when students already have considerable experience – and only after trying the exercise with the suggested resources.

Cue synopsis

Q1. An actor is sitting in chair X. A second actor enters between the flats and sits in chair Y. The actor on chair X stands up and moves around the area between table and wall, then crosses in front of the table but keeping close to it. The area to be lit is therefore that enclosed within the broken line.

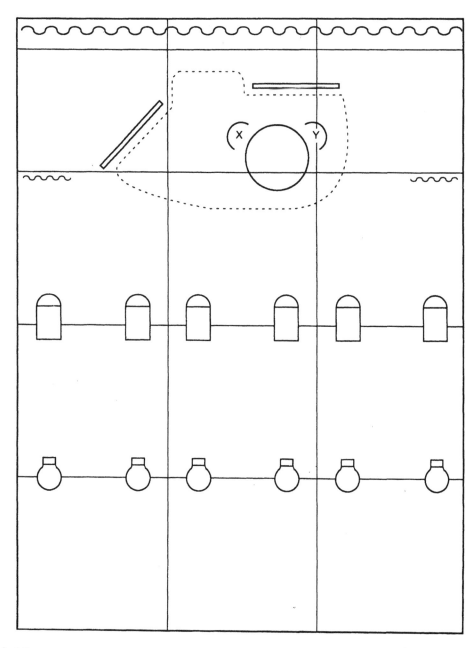

Figure P.5 Plan for Project 3

Q2. The actor sits down again and the light tightens so that audience attention is focused on both seated actors.

Possible problems

■ Remember that the broken line does not indicate an area of lit floor: it is the area within which actor faces need to be visible.
■ Actor shadows on the flats may be inevitable but they should be minimized.

Analysis of results

● Did we always see the actors as clearly as we would have wished?
● And were they sufficiently well modelled?
● Did we succeed in minimizing actor shadows on the scenic flats?
● Did we achieve the closest possible relation between face areas and floor areas?
● Were we able to keep the scene isolated, minimizing light spill on to the masking?
● Taking all the above together, did we achieve the optimum compromise between visibility, modelling and shadows?
● Given a second chance, would we rig lights in different positions?
● And/or would we focus differently?

Assessment of lighting management

● Organization of time?
● Communications?
● Equipment handling?

If automated lights available

Could the area be tightened by remote focusing in conjunction with pan and tilt?

Project 4
Creating space

Objective

To explore the use of light to create an acting space.

Setting

Four blocks of seating surround a rectangular acting area (Figure P.6).

Rig

A maximum of 20 lighting instruments may be hung anywhere on the lighting grid which extends over the acting and seating areas. Initially these should be Fresnels or PCs, but profiles may be tried after successful discovery of basic principles.

Cue synopsis

Q1. Actors should be lit everywhere within the area enclosed by the broken line.

Contraction and expansion

If possible, the number of available lights should not be reduced below 16. This project may be extended by pursuing warm and cool toning. This is still possible within the nominated 20 lighting instrument maximum, but another 6 instruments could be allowed. If the warm/cool atmospheric option is not the subject of experiment, there should certainly be a discussion of possible methods.

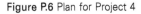

Figure P.6 Plan for Project 4

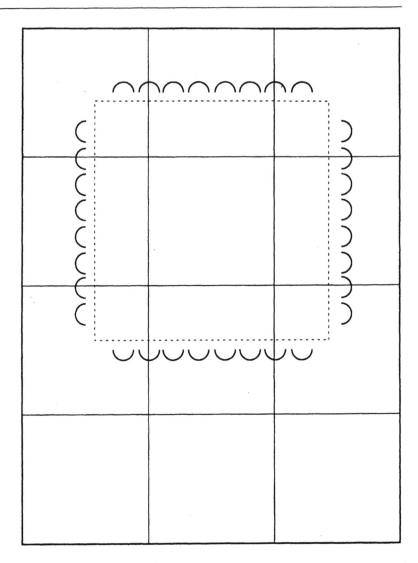

Possible problems

- The face of an actor standing close to the front row of the audience on the perimeter of the acting area (as indicated by the broken line) should be fully lit, both when playing towards the adjacent block of audience and when playing across the acting area to the opposite block of audience.
- Light should not shine into the eyes of the audience, although spill on to the audience below eye level may be acceptable if it causes neither distraction nor discomfort.
- Theatre-in-the-round is generally agreed to be very democratic, with each block of audience equally important: every member of the audience should experience a similar quality of lighting.

Analysis of results

- Did we always see the actors as clearly as we would have wished? Could we clearly see the faces of actors standing close to each front row of the audience and playing to that block of audience – and (especially) playing across the acting area to the opposite block of audience?
- Was light shining into the eyes of members of the audience?
- Were the actors sufficiently well modelled?
- Was the lighting quality similar for all blocks of audience?
- Given a second chance, would we rig lights in different positions?
- And/or would we focus differently?
- Would we have liked more equipment and, if so, how would we have used it?

Assessment of lighting management

- Organization of time?
- Communications?
- Equipment handling?

Project 5
Cool, neutral or warm

Objective

To explore the mixing of filtered light to provide a range of varying atmospheric colour from cool through neutral to warm.

Setting

A sculptural scenic object, perhaps a skeletal tree, is at position X (Figure P.7). Two actors sit in chairs at a table in position Y.

Rig

A maximum of 12 lights may be used, selected from the 6 profile and 6 focus spots on the plan, plus up to 4 additionals which may be of any available type and positioned as required. A range of about 12 filters (for example, Lee 103, 109, 117, 119, 132, 134, 136, 138, 147, 152, 161, 201; or Rosco 05, 07, 09, 21, 30, 33, 54, 63, 67, 85, 371, 388) is available from which a choice of not more than 6 may be made.

Contraction and expansion

It is just possible to achieve the objectives of this exercise with 8 lights and this should be regarded as the absolute minimum. Reduce in the order: profiles 2 and 5, focus spots 2 and 5, profiles 3 and 4, focus 3 and 4. In the interests of sharp thinking and clean lighting, the rig should not be expanded beyond 16.

Cue synopsis

Q1. The scene begins happily.
Q2. Imperceptibly the mood becomes less cheerful.

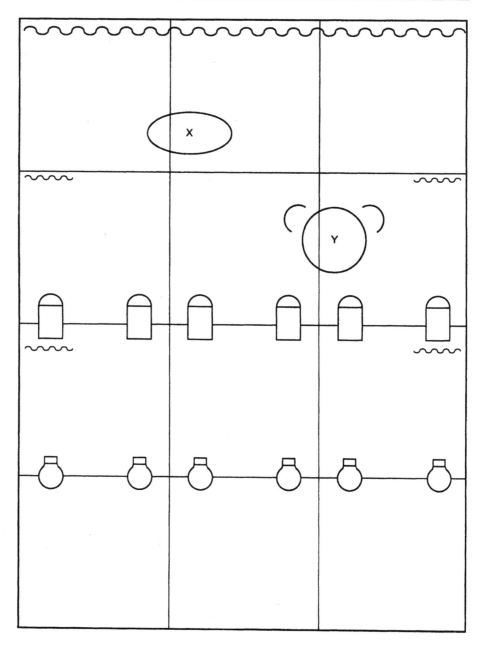

Figure P.7 Plan for Project 5

Q3. Gradually the atmosphere saddens and the relations between the two actors become distinctly chilly.

Possible problems

■ Clarity is important: beware the muddy light which can result from excessive general dimming.
■ Unless the changes are smoothly subtle, there is a danger that the light may distract from the acting rather than support it.

Analysis of results

● Did the light convey atmosphere as fully as we hoped? How well did the atmospheric change on the scenery work – and how well the change on the actors? Were the changes on set and actors well integrated?
● Did the colour palette provide everything hoped for? Did the filters enhance the colour pigments in scenery and costumes?
● Was the scenery generally enhanced by the light? Was it well sculpted – or flattened?
● Did we always see the actors as clearly as we would have wished? Were they sufficiently well sculpted?
● Was the acting area sufficiently tightly selected?
● Given a second chance, what would we do differently? Would we change the instrument positions – and/or the filters?

Assessment of lighting management

● Organization of time?
● Communications?
● Equipment handling?

If automated lights available

Could scroller or integral colour changing assist in controlling the mood?

Project 6
Atmospheric space

Objective

To explore simultaneous control of space and atmosphere.

Setting

The stage is masked by black drapes as shown (Figure P.8). There is a table and two chairs.

Rig

There are 12 lights, 6 profiles and 6 focus, on the grid. Up to a further 8 of any available type may be hung as required.

Contraction and expansion

If equipment is short, reduce the permitted additionals to 6, then remove rigged lights in the sequence 2 and 5 from the profiles, then 2 and 5 from the focus spots. The number of additionals should not be increased much beyond 10 or 12.

If time is short, it is possible, although not particularly desirable, for three designers to work simultaneously – one dealing with each area.

Cue synopsis

Q1. The area around the table is lit. It is quite cosy. She is sitting in the prompt side (PS: actors' left) chair. After a moment he enters from opposite prompt (OP: actors' right) and crosses quickly to the table where they embrace. She is evidently pleased to see him. During the ensuing scene they sit in both chairs or move around the table but remain quite close to it – as close as they can without feeling

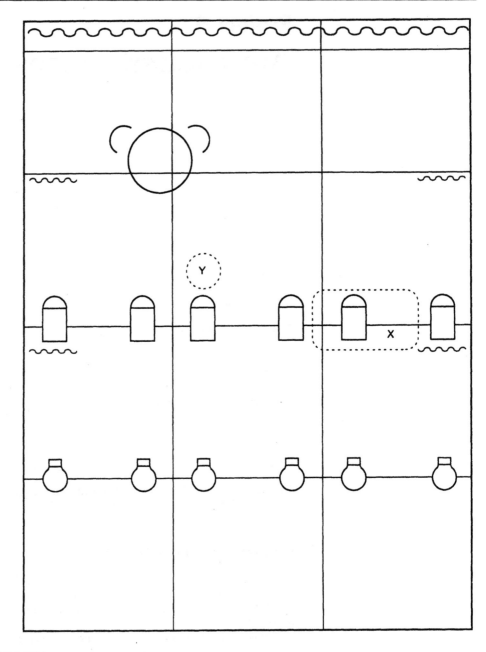

Figure P.8 Plan for Project 6

uncomfortable.

Q2. As they remember ... the emotional content of the scene cools somewhat.

Q3. A flashback to their first meeting, played by another two actors in the area X downstage. Perhaps a bit dreamlike?

Q4. After the flashback, the action returns to the table area.

Q5. He storms out. She moves downstage towards the audience (position Y) for a short soliloquy which ends with a tear before...

Q6. Fade to blackout as the scene ends.

Possible problems

■ Keeping areas tight, separate and distinct.
■ Avoiding light spill on the black masking.
■ Supporting the difference between now and flashback.

Analysis of results

● Did the light support the action as fully as we hoped? Did the palette of lights provide everything desired?
● Did we get our priorities right?
● Was the contrast between reality and flashback positive yet credible?
● Was the lighting around the table sufficiently tightly selected? Were the actors clearly visible and sufficiently modelled? And were they supported by changes of atmosphere?
● Was the flashback sufficiently dreamlike? If not, was this a fault of angle, or colour, or texture?
● Did we maintain a good visual balance over the stage as the action shifted between the three areas?
● Given a second chance, what would we do differently? Would we change the concept – or its practical implementation?

Assessment of lighting management

● Organization of time?
● Communications?
● Equipment handling?

If automated lights available

Could scroller or integral colour changing alter the emotional atmosphere? Does a moving beam, perhaps with a simultaneous colour change, help the transition to flashback?

Project 7
Musical space

Objective

To explore lighting for dance and song.

Setting

The stage is bare with an option of neutral masking or a sky cloth at the back (Figure P.9). The acting area, as indicated by the broken line, should be raised on low (e.g. 150 mm or 6 in) rostra, if available, and could be painted. If painted specially, use plain white, then add a spatter of various colours after several lighting designers have attempted the project.

Rig

There are 12 lights as shown and a further 8 may be used: if possible, the available choices should include parcans. (These numbers do not include three-colour floodlighting which should be made available for a sky cloth, if used.)

Contraction and expansion

It would be difficult to benefit from this project if resources were reduced below 15 instruments. On the other hand, the upper limit is determined only by the experience of those involved: an excess of lights can become counterproductive in the hands of an inexperienced explorer. It is possible to carry out this exercise in silence, or each designer may be offered the opportunity to select suitable music.

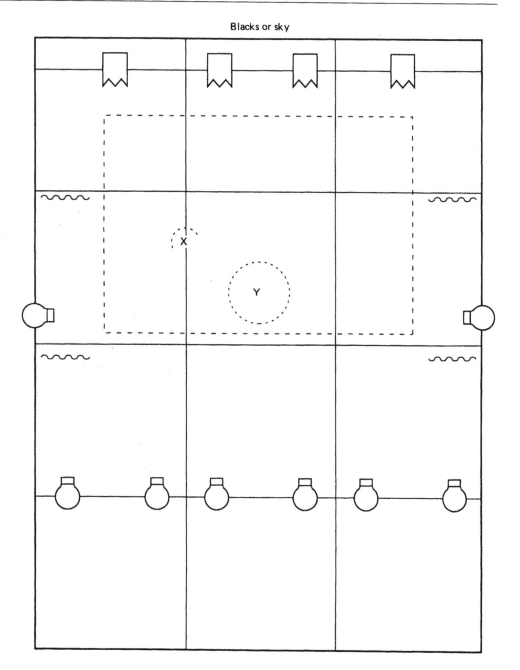

Figure P.9 Plan for Project 7

Cue synopsis

Q1. When the audience enter, a light dresses the stage.

Q2. The show opens with a dance sequence of at least 3 minutes. Ten dancers enter gradually, first one, then another, and so on – sometimes singly, occasionally in pairs, possibly one group of three. The dance gradually increases in its intensity and gets louder. The light grows with the build in the dance. It might be one long build or a sequence of cues.

Q3. There is a drum break. The dancers freeze, turn their backs on the audience and raise their arms in the air in a trembling movement.

Q4. End of drum break. They turn round and hit the audience with the first song number of the show – it is a full-bash out-front number.

Q5. At the end of the song there is a climax (applause . . . applause . . .).

Q6. During the applause, the dancers drift off. As they go, one of them places a chair (X marks the spot) and by the end of the exit (about 8 seconds) this chair is isolated for a sad song.

Q7. But the song cheers up.

Q8. And the singer moves downstage centre to finish the song (position Y).

Choreographer's note

Much of the positioning of dancers in the opening sequence is flexible and I will be happy to respond to the lighting designer's visual ideas. I do not think that the dance really needs a lot of flicker, flash and chase movement from the lights. However, I am prepared to keep an open mind, provided that any movement is not random but really linked to the music and the dance.

Possible problems

■ Beware a pre-show dressing light that is so beautifully interesting that the stage never looks so good again during the performance.

■ Beware too much too soon, or too little too late.

■ Remember that 3 minutes is a long time in dance.

Analysis of results

● Did the light help to sustain the long development of the opening dance sequence?

● Did it match the dramatic change of dance style at the drum break?

● And did it match the dramatic change from dance to song?

● Were the dancers well sculpted?

● And were the singers' faces sufficiently visible?

● Did the light sustain an atmosphere to match the music?

● Did we isolate the solo singer successfully?

● Did we match the moods of the song, shifting from sad to happy with appropriate subtlety?

● In judging priorities, did we achieve the optimum balance between dance, full-stage singing, and solo singing?

- Given a second chance, what would we do differently? Would we provide more sculpting – or more colour? Would we have a different rig balance between front, top, back and side lighting?

Assessment of lighting management

- Organization of time?
- Communications?
- Equipment handling?

If automated lights available

Could there be scope in this project for colour changing, focus changing and, if the available equipment is sufficiently versatile, gobo changing?

Project 8
Areas and atmospheres

Objective

To explore tight selection of areas in an atmosphere of romantically heightened moonlight, sunlight and lamplight.

Setting

An excerpt from a romantic opera, probably written towards the end of the nineteenth century, full of soaring melodies with high held notes at the climaxes. A tower stands just off centre with steps descending to the stage via an intermediate level (Figures P.10, P.11). There are black legs at the side of the stage and the option of blacks or a plain sky cloth at the back.

Rig

Up to 20 lights (including the 8 shown on the plan) may be hung from the grid or used on stands (plus floodlighting for a sky cloth if used).

Contraction and expansion

It is difficult, although just possible, to meet the objectives of this project with fewer than 10 lights. Any increase above the suggested 20 should only be as an extension of the project and after a good case has been argued in favour of the extra.

Cue synopsis

Preset. When the audience enter, they see the shape of what may be a tower.

Q1. With the aid of dramatic rumblings from the orchestra, the tower becomes a more insistent focus for our attention. He appears at the top, somewhat agitated, looks furtively around, then comes down the

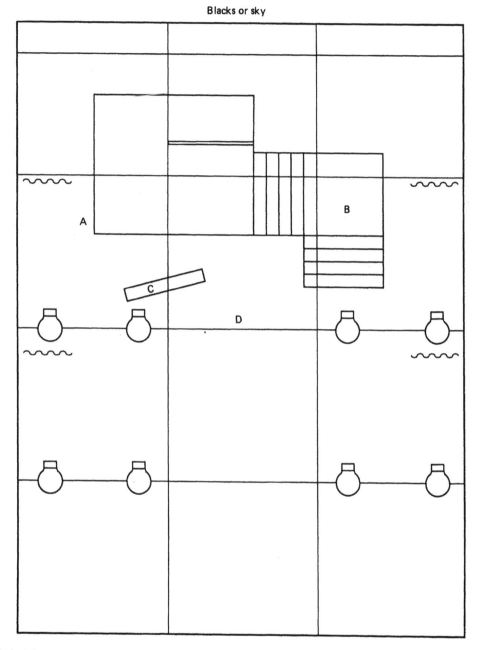

Figure P.10 Plan for Project 8

Figure P.11 The set may be constructed from available stock rostrum and step units, with considerable scope for variation in the proportions. If possible, the shape should be softened and textured by draping with rough material: sacking or camouflage netting are effective

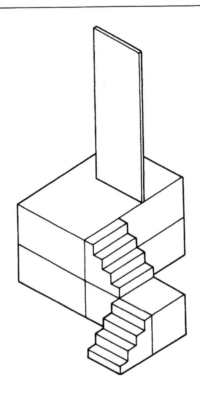

steps. He is obviously frightened of being seen. He ends up hiding at the side of the tower (position A).

Q2. She now appears at the top of the tower (in the same position as he did). She is carrying a lantern and is looking for him. She holds the lantern up and looks down from the tower, trying to see if he is below.

Q3. She now comes down the steps, pausing for a moment as she turns (position B) to once again look below her, then having given a quick token look round at the foot of the steps, she crosses to the bench, sits (putting the lantern on the ground at her feet) and starts to sing a sad song (position C).

Q4. During the song, dawn begins to break rather gently and romantically.

Q5. She gets a bit more passionate about her love for him, stands up and comes to centre (position D). Perhaps the sun rises a bit more.

Q6. Realizing that she loves him, he comes forward from hiding. They embrace and go into a rapturous duet. This change to happiness conveniently coincides with the progress of the rising sun.

Q7. The duet ends in triumphant climax, he leads her off to a new life, exiting downstage left (PS).

Director's note

I am uncertain whether we should see this tower against black curtains or a sky and I am prepared to be led by the lighting designer. The light, particularly in its direction, should relate to its sources with sufficient logic as not to put too much stress on credibility. However, in keeping with the romantic excesses of the music, there is considerable opportunity for quite dramatic contrasts of light and shade – together with a heightened use of colour.

Possible problems

■ The audience must, of course, be able to see the hero in the moonlight, but the lighting should have enough credibility for us to believe that he could be unseen by the heroine (or by her father/ husband/lover or whoever, if the tower is overlooked).

■ But the main credibility problem is likely to be contriving a candle or oil light that appears to be sourced by the lantern.

Analysis of results

● Did the light support the action as fully as we hoped?
● Was the lighting style appropriate – and consistent? Was it fully integrated? Were its priorities right?
● Was the light too naturalistic? Or should it have been more naturalistic?
● Could it have contributed more to the atmosphere?
● Did the choice of colour filters support the atmosphere? And did they enrich the scenery and costumes?
● Was the scenery generally enhanced by the light? Was it well sculpted – or flattened? Were the mechanics of its construction disguised – or exposed?
● How close did the final result match what we set out to achieve? Did the palette of focused lights provide everything hoped for?
● Were we flexible in developing ideas or did we stick too rigidly with our first concept?
● Was there more compromise than anticipated?
● Was each instrument in the rig able to do its planned job? Or did scenery ever get in the way? If the latter, should our planning have been able to anticipate this?
● Should the acting areas have been more tightly selected?
● Did we always see the actors as clearly as we would have wished? And were they sufficiently well sculpted?
● Given a second chance, what would we do differently? Would we change the concept – or its practical implementation?

Assessment of lighting management

● Organization of time?
● Communications?
● Equipment handling?

If automated lights available

Is it possible to track the candle with a moving light? Or would it seem too much like a follow spot? Can a slow scroll or integral changing colour help the rising sun?

Project 9
The magic of gauze

Objective

To explore the technique of dissolving (or 'bleeding') through a gauze from the picture painted on the gauze to the picture set behind.

Setting

A painted gauze hangs at the front of the stage (Figure P.12). Blacks are available to back this gauze. (The gauze and backs should be capable of being flown if possible, otherwise they are moved on tab tracks). A painted backcloth (or sky cloth or blacks) hangs at the back of the stage.

Rig

In addition to the 15 lights shown on the plan, up to a further 15 may be rigged where required. A small hand-held smoke gun (e.g. Minimist or Scotty) may be made available on request. Flood coverage (three-colour if possible) should be available for the backcloth or sky option.

Contraction and expansion

Although 30 lights are suggested, carefully planned pairing could reduce the dimmer requirement to 20 channels. It is difficult to carry out the full exercise with fewer than about 20 lights. If less equipment is available, or time is particularly short, omit the mood change in front of the gauze and the move forward after the front gauze is flown or tracked out. The project then becomes feasible with a minimum of 12 lights. Extras should only be allowed after the maximum possibilities have been extracted from the suggested 30, and a clear need established for specific experiment from additional angles.

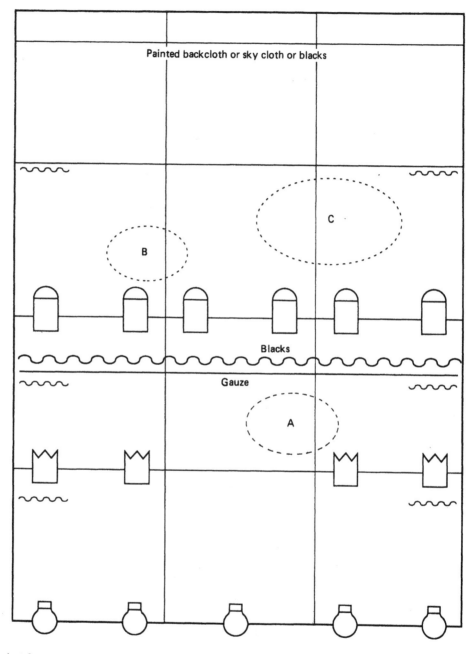

Figure P.12 Plan for Project 9

Cue synopsis

Q1. The gauze is lit attractively during a short cheerful overture.

Q2. With a change of music the mood becomes sinister, and a couple of actors (in sombre costumes of dark muted browns and greys) are lit when standing in area A.

Q3. As the actors exit, the picture on the front of the gauze disappears and we see an actor (in a white shirt and dark trousers) standing in area B.

Q4. The scene gradually builds with some light on the backcloth and four dancers (in bright multicoloured frocks) become visible in area C.

Q5. The gauze flies (or tracks) out and the cast move forward with a cheerful song and dance. (Note: the gauze goes about half a minute after we have first bled through it.)

Possible problems

■ Avoiding seeing through the gauze when it is lit from the front.
■ Avoiding showing up the inevitable wrinkles in the gauze.
■ Minimizing shadows on the gauze of actors standing in front of it.
■ Lighting the actor in position B, close to the gauze.
■ Smooth timing.

Analysis of results

● Did our palette of focused lights provide everything hoped for?
● Could it have contributed more to the atmosphere?
● Was the choice of colour filters atmospherically supportive? – and did they enhance the scenery and costumes?
● Were the gauze and backcloth generally enhanced by the light? – supporting any painted perspective? – without showing creases?
● Should the acting areas have been more tightly selected?
● Did we always see the actors as clearly as we would have wished? – and were they sufficiently well sculpted?
● Given a second chance, what would we do differently? – lighting from different angles? – and/or with different filters?

Assessment of lighting management

● Organization of time?
● Communications?
● Equipment handling?

If automated lights available

Would a scrolled or integral colour change assist the mood change on the gauze?

Project 10

Non-orthodox minimalism

Objective

To explore non-orthodox methods of lighting, using a minimum number of sources.

Setting

The rear of the acting area is defined by a plain monochrome (pale white, cream or grey) wall (Figure P.13). On PS (actors' left) this rear wall joins a side wall with a series of windows, preferably with louvred shutters. These window flats run up and down stage at a slight angle and join another flat, with a practical door, running on and off stage. The acting area can be used as both an interior and an exterior: in different scenes we are either inside or outside the house.

Rig

The aim is to use high powered sources to simulate the natural sources of sun and moon, allowing the surfaces in the scenic environment to reflect as do surfaces in real life – and to let any artificial sources provide adequate light without reinforcement by discreet spotlighting.

The only standard theatre lighting instruments likely to be of use in this project are 2 kW or 2.5 kW Fresnels, and perhaps 1 kW floods. If possible, some television or film studio luminaires should be available including a 5 kW tungsten or HMI discharge Fresnel. The particular instruments actually used will depend upon what can be acquired. Only one really powerful source is required, plus a couple of smaller ones. These instruments do not need to offer a highly sophisticated control of the light beam: as happens in nature, much of the control of the light will be in the way it is channelled by objects which form part of the environment. Sheets of board or pieces of spare scenery may be used to shape the beam of a primitive source when mounted out of sight. Indeed, subject to observing

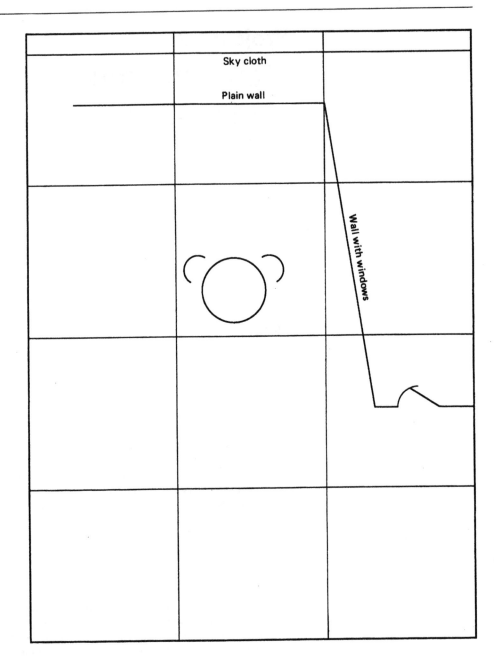

Figure P.13 Plan for Project 10

the strictest safety precautions, there may be scope for adapting unlikely non-theatre luminaires for stage use.

Contraction and expansion

As the resources specified for this project are already minimal, there is no scope for reduction. However, since perception of light intensity is largely dependent upon balance, high powered sources are not absolutely essential: although a source of at least 2 kW is highly desirable, experiments with 1 kW are worth pursuing if nothing brighter is available.

Development possibilities centre on renting or borrowing a really high powered HMI studio Fresnel.

The scene and cue sequence may also be used with orthodox lighting techniques: however, it is preferable that such an exercise should follow rather than precede an exploration of minimalism.

Cue synopsis

Q1. Set dressing.

Q2. Fade to blackout and houselights out.

Q3. Build day interior. Sunlight through windows (also outside door when opened).

Q4. Fade to blackout.

Q5. Build night exterior. Lights on inside house.

Q6. Fade to blackout.

Q7. Build night interior. Moonlight through windows. Two actors at table are lit by a practical lamp which either stands on the table or hangs above it.

Q8. Light becomes slightly sinister.

Q9. As actors rise from chairs and grapple in the table area, light becomes very sinister and unnatural.

Q10. One actor exits, leaving other slumped over table.

Q11. Fade to blackout.

Possible problems

- Reliance on reflected light from scenic surfaces to provide sufficient illumination on the sides of faces not directly lit from the key source – particularly in respect of helping the actors project beyond the first two or three rows of audience.
- Insufficient control of reflected light.
- Contriving accurately repeatable smooth mechanical dimming for sources which cannot be dimmed electrically.

Analysis of results

- Did the light provide as much support as we hoped?
- Were we flexible in developing ideas rather than sticking rigidly to our first concept?
- Was there more compromise than anticipated?

● Was the lighting style appropriate, consistent, and fully integrated with the action? Were its priorities right?
● Was the light too naturalistic? Or should it have been more naturalistic?
● Could it have contributed more to the atmosphere?
● Was the colour supportive?
● Did we always see the actors as clearly as we would have wished? And were they sufficiently well sculpted?
● Given a second chance, what would we do differently? Would we change the concept – or its practical implementation?

Assessment of lighting management

● Organisation of time?
● Communications?
● Equipment handling?

Project 11
Figaro's garden

Objective

To explore the problems of providing enough visibility for the audience to understand the action, while maintaining the atmospheric credibility of a moonlit garden which is sufficiently dark and shadowy for mistaken identities to be feasible.

The project

The project is based on the final act of Mozart's opera *The Marriage of Figaro*. While it is possible to carry out the project from the information given here, a preliminary study of the opera is highly recommended. This should include a detailed analysis of the last act, paying particular attention to the mistaken identities. (The available recordings are in the original Italian, but are normally boxed with English translations of the libretto.)

Setting

The scene is a garden (Figure P.14). For this project it is represented by three foliage arches – set downstage left, downstage right, and upstage centre. There is an option to back the set with a sky cloth or neutral blacks: perhaps individuals in the group should choose their preferred alternative. The simplicity of the three arches could possibly be augmented by some trellises or by some stonework such as a crumbling statue. However, it should not become too detailed or realistic: the objective is to create a garden ambience with light.

All the critical action happens in the area downstage centre (marked by the broken line). However, eavesdroppers appear from time to time at the downstage arches and immediately upstage of them. In these positions, they should be sufficiently well lit for the audience to recognize who they are, although it is not necessary for their faces to be seen with full clarity.

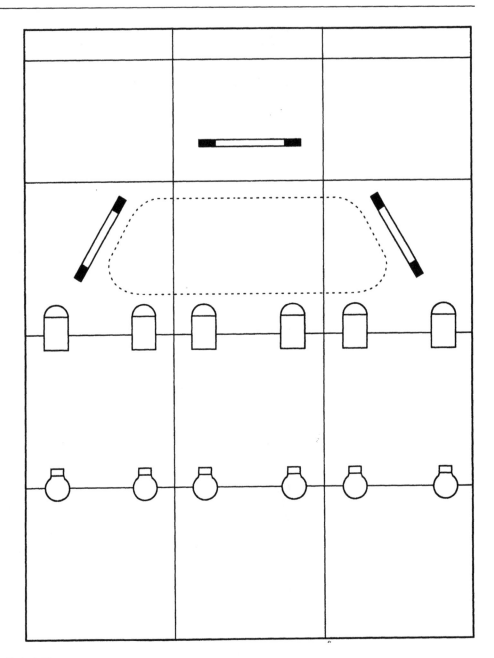

Figure P.14 Plan for Project 11

Rig

Up to 30 lights may be used, including the 12 on the plan.

Contraction and expansion

The project is feasible with a dozen lights but resources should preferably not be reduced much below 20 (cut permitted additionals to 10 or 12 and remove lights 2 and 5 from each of the bars).

Cue synopsis

It is possible to make many subtle rebalancing changes, either subconscious or motivated by a moon which is hidden by clouds from time to time. However, the basic cues are:

Q1. Establish idea of shadowy darkness with fairly tight visibility down centre for first (Barbarina) aria.
Q2. Very slow build towards end of this aria, cheating the light up to the main state.
Q3. General entry with lanterns at beginning of resolution of the plot.
Q4. Slight build on Countess entry through upstage arch.
Q5. Build on final ensemble (everyone lined up, singing out front to audience).

Possible problems

■ The darkness is such that individual actors mistake each other's identity, yet the audience can see who is who. It is a matter of balance: lightness and darkness are relative.
■ The words for Susanna's aria say that the moon is not yet out. But without some suggestion of moonlight, it is difficult to provide light and shade for the complex intrigues prior to this aria. Moreover, the presence of some discreet moon helps to provide sculptural modelling for actors and scenery.
■ Unrelieved blue can be very tiring to the eyes: a little warmth may make an impact without being noticed.

Analysis of results

● Did the light support the action and music as fully as we hoped?
● How close did the final result match what we set out to achieve? Did the palette of focused lights provide everything hoped for?
● Was the lighting style appropriate, consistent, and fully integrated? Were its priorities right?
● Was the light too naturalistic? Or should it have been more naturalistic?
● Could it have contributed more to the atmosphere?
● Was the choice of colour filters atmospherically supportive? Did they enhance the scenery and costumes?

- Was the scenery generally enhanced by the light? Was it well sculpted – or flattened? Were its construction mechanics disguised – or exposed?
- Should the acting areas have been more tightly selected?
- Did we always see the actors as clearly as we would have wished? And were the actors well sculpted? Yet were mistaken identities credible?
- Given a second chance, what would we do differently? Would we change instrument positions, filters, focus, balance?

Assessment of lighting management

- Organization of time?
- Communications?
- Equipment handling?

If automated lights available

Would they help the entry with lanterns?

Project 12
Macbeth's witches

Objective

To explore the lighting of a highly atmospheric scene involving phenomena which appear to be supernatural.

Setting

The second witch's scene from *Macbeth* (Act IV Scene I). The acting area is surrounded by black drapes (Figure P.15). The scene, assembled from found objects including a 'cauldron', and the manner in which the various apparitions and kings appear, are devised by the lighting group collaborating on the project.

Rig

A maximum of 20 lights including the 10 specified (plus flooding for optional sky cloth) may be used.

Contraction and expansion

A reduction in the number of lights down to about a dozen is feasible but not recommended. Any extension should concentrate on developing the project rather than just allowing more lights, e.g. by making effects projectors available or repeating in a theatre-in-the-round format.

After lighting the scene as spoken drama, it might be interesting to repeat the project using the same scene in Verdi's opera based on the original Shakespeare. This would involve the added dimensions of very atmospheric music and a trio of witches expanded into singing and dancing choruses.

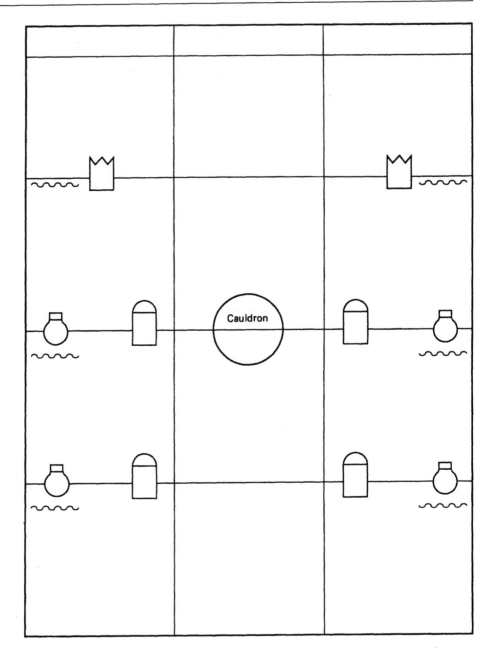

Figure P.15 Plan for Project 12

Cue synopsis

Q1. The three witches at the cauldron.
Q2. Enter Hecate.
Q3. Exit Hecate.
Q4. Enter Macbeth.
Q5. First Apparition (armed head) appears.
Q6. Apparition disappears.
Q7. Second Apparition (bloody child) appears.
Q8. Apparition disappears.
Q9. Third Apparition (child crowned with tree in hand) appears.
Q10. Apparition disappears.
Q11. Show of eight kings.
Q12. Show of kings vanishes.
Q13. Witches exit.
Q14. Lennox enters.
Q15. Exit – end of scene.

Possible problems

■ Establishing an atmosphere which has some basis in reality but where supernatural happenings do not seem too incredible.
■ Staging the apparitions and show of kings. (Props, puppets, ballet and projection are some of the methods that have been used in productions.)

Analysis of results

● Did the light provide as much support as we hoped?
● Were we flexible in developing ideas as we observed the way in which the scenic elements responded to light?
● Was the lighting style appropriate, consistent, and fully integrated? Were its priorities right?
● Was the light too naturalistic? Or should it have been more naturalistic?
● Did the atmosphere support the supernatural happenings? Was the choice of colour filters supportive?
● And did these colours enhance the scenery and costumes?
● Was the scenery generally enhanced by the light? Was it well sculpted – or flattened? Were its mechanics disguised – or exposed?
● Should the acting areas have been more tightly selected?
● Did we always see the actors as clearly as we would have wished? And were they sufficiently well sculpted?
● Given a second chance, what would we do differently? Would we arrange the scene differently, or the general lighting, and/or the staging of the supernatural phenomena?

Assessment of lighting management

● Organization of time?
● Communications?
● Equipment handling?

If automated lights available

Would beam movement assist the supernatural atmosphere? And perhaps draw attention to each apparition? Could sequential movement be used as a metaphor for the show of kings?

Project 13
Tape and light

Objective

To explore the interaction and coordination of music and light.

Setting

Assemble an environment from found objects (Figure P.16). Design a fluid lighting sequence which explores the way in which lighting may add a time dimension to our perception of sculptural objects in terms of form and atmosphere. The performance may be accompanied by any kind of sound track or by silence.

Rig

Up to 20 lights may be used, including the five marked on the plan.

Contraction and expansion

This project can be reduced to any minimum. Doing it with two lights or even just one would be a challenge – but it could be a legitimate and potentially rewarding challenge! Similarly, the expansion possibilities are virtually limitless, although the resulting palette might become increasingly difficult to mix.

Since this project results in audio-visual experiences without actor involvement, audiences need not be confined to the participating group. Performing a series of individual 'pieces' in sequence can extend the project into an exploration of many aspects of technical and personal coordination. A possible approach for, say, 12 students is:

■ Working in 3 groups of 4 people, each group producing one joint design for performance in not less than 3 and not more than 10 minutes.

■ At performance, each group to be able to set in 10 minutes and strike in 5 minutes.

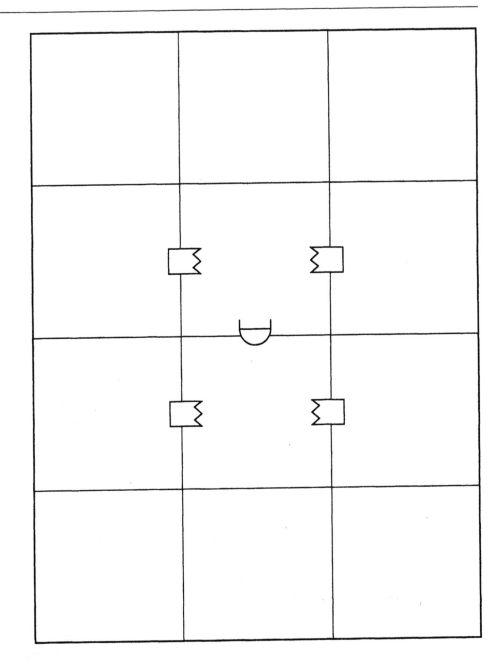

Figure P.16 Plan for Project 13

■ Rig divided into three categories: (1) lights special to each group, (2) lights which may be refocused within the 10 minute setting time and (3) lights permanently focused in a way determined by group discussion and agreement.

■ Schedule allocating sequential slots for focusing, plotting and rehearsing.

Cue synopsis

For this project, the cue sequence is designed by each designer to suit his or her own scenario.

Possible problems

■ This project has no actors – a rare occurrence in theatre. Will this absence of actors be a liberating experience?

■ With no dialogue and no action, audience concentration is acutely focused on sound and light. Under these circumstances, 3 minutes can seem an eternity and use up a lot of light changes.

■ Combining a sequence of pieces into a single performance is likely to involve priorities and compromises.

Analysis of results

● How closely did the final result match what we set out to achieve?

● Were we flexible in observing the response of the scenic objects to light and developing our ideas accordingly?

● Did the palette of focused lights provide everything hoped for?

● Was the light fully integrated with the sound?

● Did our use of light take full advantage of the absence of actors – enabling us to concentrate on sculptural modelling and atmosphere?

● Did the choice of colour filters support the scene?

● Given a second chance, what might we change: the set, the sound, the light? Or would we devise a completely different scenario?

Assessment of lighting management

● Organization of time?
● Communications?
● Equipment handling?

If automated lights available

Perhaps this project could be totally structured around beams that move and change colour?

Project 14

The twenty spot opera house

Objective

To explore the use of minimum resources to light a show with demanding requirements.

Project basis

This final project is one which is difficult to attempt without access to painted cloths and gauzes, preferably flown but possibly tracked. Nevertheless it has been included as an example of a real situation which demonstrates what has to be achieved (and can be achieved) with minimum resources if the performance is to take place.

The project is based on a performance of Handel's opera *Teseo* at the Siena Festival in 1985. The production toured scenery, cast and orchestra but adapted its lighting plot to the available equipment. The schedule was:

Day One
Morning: Carpenter and stage management get in and set up.
Evening: Stage rehearsal.
Light designer arrives, discovers equipment and draws plan.

Day Two
9.00 Rig lighting.
10.00 Orchestra seating (focus FOH).
10.15 Dress rehearsal, no lights (focus stage during break).
4.00 Plot.
8.30 Performance.

There was a memory board (Strand Duet). Ten 1 kW PC spotlights were mounted front of house, five each side, on the outwardly curving ends of the upper box tier of the bell-shaped auditorium. They provided an excellent face angle with all instruments able to cover any part of the stage. A further ten 1 kW PCs were available to rig as required using wooden spot bars hung as required. Wooden booms and ladders were available on request. There were no barndoors, only French flags (i.e. single leaves on jointed arms which could be attached to the spotlight yokes). Over the stage were three three-colour battens, but with only enough frames for the upstage batten which had primary red, deep blue and amber filters.

Setting

The set, designed by Terence Emery and based on flown cloths and gauzes painted in eighteenth-century perspective style, looked very well in the restored eighteenth-century Bibiena Theatre. A fairly massive false proscenium framed a set of treads leading to a 600 mm (2 ft) high rostrum (Figure P.17). This false proscenium, about 5.5 m (18 ft) wide, was set about 2.5 m (8 ft) from the front of the stage. Two three-dimensional chandeliers hung in this downstage area (Figure P.18). All other scenery was cloths or gauzes dropped on to the rostrum area. They were beautifully painted and took light well (Figure P.19). Colouring was yellows/beiges for the stone, bluey-greens for the garden and island, blue clouds with a bit of gold. All the acting area in front of the treads was used – and the treads themselves. Although the actors used all the rostrum, they tended to move to top centre when they had anything important to sing.

Resolution of *Teseo*'s complex plot involves several devices of classical mythology, including a conflagration and appearances of deities (in this production, by dissolving through gauzes). These occurrences form part of the cue synopsis.

Rig

This project is an adaptation of that day in Siena. The plan shows ten fixed PCs FOH. The decisions required are:

- how to colour and where to focus the ten PCs FOH
- where to hang, colour and focus the other ten PCs.

Contraction and expansion

Reduction in the number of lights is just too cruel to be contemplated! Although the production could be expanded to use the full resources of an international opera house, it might be more interesting to consider what one might do with just an extra ten lights.

Cue synopsis

Q1.   (5s)   House tabs out to reveal act drop in and chandeliers at stage level. Dim. Cold.
Q2.   (12s) Footmen light chandeliers which then fly.
Q3.   (5s)   Act drop flys into temple. Warm.
Q4.   (5s)   Arch cut in. Rebalance.
Q5.   (5s)   Down to scene change light.
Q6.   (5s)   Build bright sunny for palace.

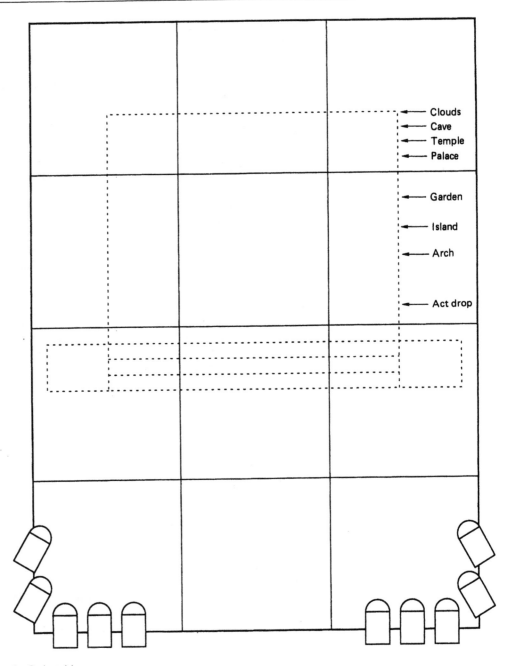

Figure P.17 Plan for Project 14

Figure P.18 False proscenium

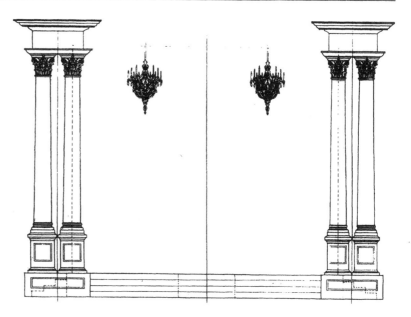

Figure P.19 Palace cloth

Q7.   (20s) Check apron.
Q8.   (5s)   Act drop in (as Q2 state).
Q9.   (5s)   Act drop flys – into palace and arch. Coldish.
Q10.   (30s) Warm up. Quite bright.
Q11.   (15s) Arch out. Very bright.
Q12.   (45s) To blues.
Q13.   (5s)   Act drop in.
Q14.   House tabs in.

Interval
Q15.   (5s)   Tabs out. Act drop lit.
Q16.   (5s)   Act drop away into garden. Daylight.
Q17.   (30s) Cross-fade to blues.
Q18.   (5s)   Fly garden to reveal cave.
Q19.   (5s)   Act drop in. Dressing.
Q20.   (5s)   Act drop out. Into palace. Warm.
Q21.   (5s)   Palace fly to reveal cave. Cool.
Q22.   (5s)   Cross to island gauze. Warm.
Q23.   (5s)   Medea appears behind gauze.
Q24.   (5s)   Medea vanishes.
Q25.   (10s) Lose apron.
Q26.   (5s)   Cross as act drop in (blue dressing).
Q27.   (5s)   Act drop out. Blues.
Q28.   (5s)   Cross to warm as arch in and island out.
Q29.   (12s) Cross to blues.
Q30.   (5s)   Add fire.
Q31.   (10s) Fire out. Cross to Minerva behind gauze section in cloud
              cloth.
Q32.   (10s) Build warms.
Q33.   (10s) Act drop in.
Q34.   (5s)   Act drop out for calls.
Q35.   (5s)   Fade to blackout and house tabs in.

Possible problems

■ This project is mainly about priorities.
■ The major and obvious problem is how to do so much with so little.
■ There are Medea and Minerva appearances to be solved.
■ And a scene has to go up in flames.
■ Will the chandeliers (which are alight throughout) help or get in the
  way?

Analysis of results

● Did the light support the production as fully as it could?
● Was there more (or less!) compromise than anticipated?
● Did we get the priorities right?
● Was the lighting style appropriate – and consistent?
● Could it have contributed more to the atmosphere? Was the choice of
  colour filters atmospherically supportive? Did it enhance the scenery
  and costumes?

- Did we always see the actors as clearly as we would have wished?
- And were they sufficiently well sculpted?
- Given a second chance, what would we do differently? Would we alter light positions, or filters?

Assessment of light management

- Organization of time?
- Communications?
- Equipment handling?

If automated lights available

Is refocusing the answer to lighting managment in a twenty spot opera house?

Project 15
A traverse stage

Setting

The audience sit on two sides of an acting area. There is an important-looking chair at one end and a small raised platform at the other. Entrances are made from behind a darkly neutral flat standing on this platform. The backing could be black masking, possibly partly opened to show a small section of sky or perhaps another flat.

Rig

Any positions may be chosen for lighting instruments which should not exceed about twenty.

Contraction and expansion

Achieving smooth sculptural visibility throughout the acting area can take about sixteen instruments. The minimum, even for a barely acceptable patchy cover, is probably four. It can be a rather useful exercise to discover the optimum deployment of various instrument numbers within this range.

Cue synopsis

Q1. A woman enters from behind the screen on the platform. She descends the steps and walks slowly towards the chair. Who is she? There is an atmosphere of mystery. We do not see her face clearly.
Q2. She sits in the chair. We see her face.
Q3. The light gets stronger. The scene is bright and happy. A man enters and they move everywhere on the floor acting area (but do not use the platform area after the man has entered.)
Q4. The atmosphere becomes sadder. He exits.
Q5. She sits in the chair.

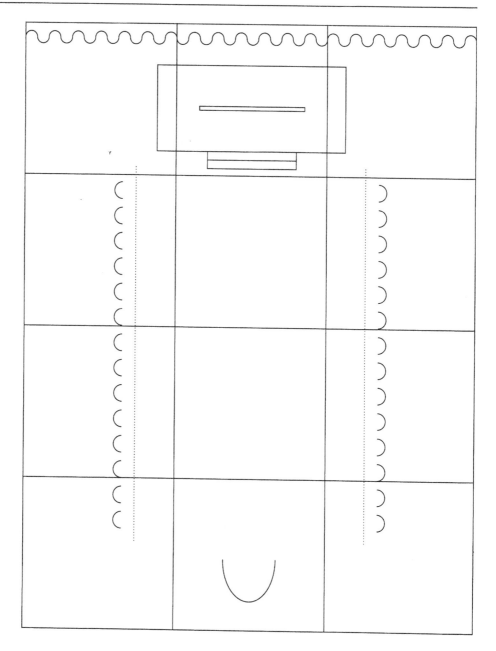

Figure P.20 Plan for Project 15

Q6. A non-realistic figure appears on the platform and makes a sign.
Q7. She rises from the chair and moves to the platform.
Q8. She exits.

Possible problems

- A small traverse stage is generally agreed to be a democratic theatre form: every member of the audience should experience a similar quality of lighting.
- If the opening and closing sequences are given excessive priority there may not be enough equipment available for the much longer fully lit sequence in the acting area.
- Particular care is required in selecting instrument positions to provide angles that light the actor satisfactorily without shining in the audience's eyes.

Analysis of results

- Did we achieve an appropriate atmosphere of mystery for the opening and closing sequences?
- Was the lighting quality similar for both blocks of audience?
- Did we always see the actors as clearly as we would have wished? Could we see the faces clearly of actors standing close to each front row of the audience, especially playing across the acting area to the opposite block of audience?
- Did any light shine into the eyes of the audience?
- How convincing was the transition to a sadder atmosphere?

Assessment of lighting management

- Organization of time?
- Communications?
- Equipment handling?

If automated lights available

Experiment with an alternative approach to the opening and closing sequences – perhaps a spreading of focus to provide a bridge from concentration on the chair to the main acting area, with a tightening when the chair again becomes dominant. It would be interesting to try a dynamic tracking as she exits – perhaps showing the way by leading rather than following. There is scope for colour scrolling, whether the scollers are fitted to conventional or automated instruments.

Project 16
Light and life

Setting

A pile of rubbish contrived from found objects which probably includes material to disguise the bodies concealed within. Audience seats may be placed in any configuration and should be considered as an integral part of the set design.

Rig

Any positions may be chosen for lighting instruments which should not exceed about twenty, but could be much less.

Contraction and expansion

It would be interesting to discover how much can be achieved with as few as three lights – and investigating the results of overlapping several textured beams.

Cue synopsis

Q1. The houselights are low and mysterious when the audience enter. Perhaps they need to be guided to their seats. The acting area appears to be occupied by a pile of rubbish.
Q2. The pile of rubbish becomes slightly more visible but the atmosphere of mystery remains.
Q3. Is there movement in the heap? Or is it an illusion?
Q4. Is it coming to life?
Q5. Perhaps the life is human?
Q6. There is a flash of lightning which illuminates a figure (? or two) for the briefest of moments.
Q7. The heap subsides and we see that it is indeed rubbish.

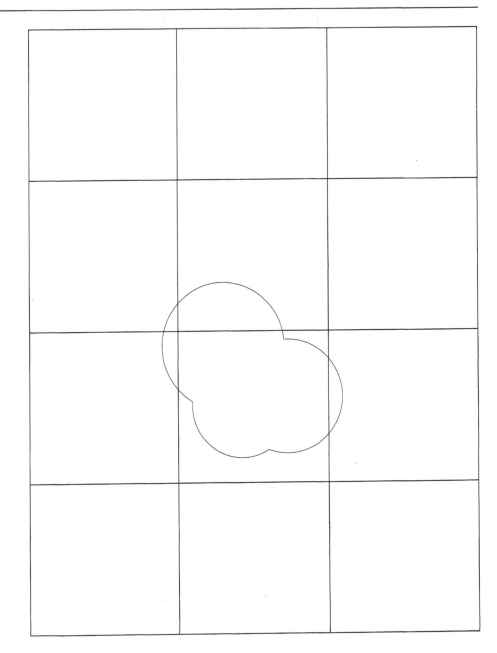

Figure P.21 Plan for Project 16

Possible problems

■ Keeping light sculptural and vibrant at low intensity levels can be difficult. Beware the mud tendency when unfiltered or pale-tinted lamps are excessively dimmed.

■ It is not easy to provide the short bursts at high intensity which are a feature of lightning, whether flashes or forks.

■ This project is particularly dependent upon sensitive timing and smooth fades.

Analysis of results

● How well did the light support the life cycle of the rubbish heap, coordinating with its movement?

● Whether naturalistic or metaphoric, was the lightning dramatically convincing?

Assessment of lighting management

● Organization of time?
● Communications?
● Equipment handling?

If automated lights available

There may be scope for tightening and opening focus. And there could be possibilities in the ability of advanced spot automated lights to soften, harden and change gobos. Wash and spot instruments with discharge lamps usually have a strobe facility which can be a useful component of lightning.

Project 17
Light as language

Objective

To explore the possibilities of light as pure visual language, rather than as a means by which people and objects are revealed, concealed and enhanced.

Setting

Using a found space and the minimum of objects (if possible, using only objects already present in the space) devise a sequence of light pictures. The sequence may be based on an unspoken narrative or be completely abstract. There are no actors and the only sounds are the movements of the audience. A trace, just a trace, of smoke may be used.

Rig

Any found space may be used. A lighting grid is not essential. Lights may be positioned by any safe methods including conventional stands and devised structures. Any source may be used: the project is not restricted to orthodox stage lighting equipment.

The project should be developed first without colour filters. After performance and analysis, it should be repeated with colour filters – perhaps incorporating new ideas with those already explored in monochrome.

Cue synopsis

The audience are drawn into the space by light. There are no seats. As the sequence unfolds, the audience are guided around the space by the light.

Possible problems

- Light is visible only when it hits an object or person.
- Light beams are barely visible in 'clean' air.

Analysis of results

- Did the lack of a scenario provide freedom or would we have been happier with some given situation to respond to (or possibly react against)?
- Did we embark on the project in a spirit of true exploration, experimenting with lights in various positions, observing the effect and relating that effect to its cause?
- To what extent, if at all, was colour an advantage?

Assessment of lighting management

- Organization of time?
- Communications?
- Equipment handling?

If automated lights available

After the project has been fully explored, in both monochrome and colour, with fixed lights, experiment with the use of moving beams to create pictures and to guide the audience. If advanced instruments are available, investigate the use of gobos and diffusion to vary the textural quality of the light.

Glossary

acting areas   Parts of the stage setting where acting is located.

backlight   Modelling light which strikes from behind to increase the illusion of depth by separating individual items of scenery from each other and separating actors from the scenic background.

bar   Horizontal tube of scaffolding diameter from which scenery or lights are suspended.

barndoors   Set of four rotatable shutters fixed as an accessory to the front of a Fresnel or PC focus spot to control spill and provide a rough shaping of the beam.

battens   (1) Lengths of floodlighting with alternating compartments wired in groups for colour mixing. (2) Lengths of timber at the tops and bottoms of cloths, or used to join flats together for flying (French flats).

beam angle   The angle of the cone of light emerging from a spotlight. More accurately the 'half peak angle' – the point in the distribution of light across the beam where intensity falls away to not less than half its maximum value, perceived by the eye as a virtually even beam.

beamlights   Instruments with no lens but with a parabolic reflector producing a parallel or near parallel beam.

blacks   Neutral masking with black curtaining – formerly of gathered velour but now more commonly of straight heavy cotton.

bleed   Replacing the picture painted on a gauze with a scene set behind by crossfading from light on the front of the gauze to light behind.

boom   Vertical tube of scaffolding diameter to which lights are bracketed by means of boom arms.

borders   Scenic or neutral horizontal strips of material hung above the stage, usually to mask flown lights and scenery.

bridges   Walkways above auditorium or stage for mounting spotlights and providing access to them for focusing.

build   (1) Increase light intensity. (2) Assemble a scene from its component parts.

channel   The path from an operator's finger on the control desk through all the circuitry to the dimmers and onward to the socket into which a light or lights have been plugged.

chase   Rapid switching of several lights in a looped sequence to give an illusion of movement.

cheating   Moving a light beam's position or intensity so slowly that the audience are not consciously aware of the change.

check   Decrease in light intensity.

colour filters   See **filters**.

correction filters   See **filters**.

cue   The signal which initiates any change on the stage – e.g. fly cue, light cue.

cue synopsis   Listing of all the lighting cues in a production showing timing, position in script and intended effect.

DBO   Dead blackout of all the light on the stage, usually as a snap – i.e. with a fade time of zero seconds.

diffusers   See **filters**.

dimming   Progressive smooth reduction of light from 100% brightness to 0% (blackout).

discharge lamps   Lamps which have no filament but generate high intensity light by electricity jumping the gap between two electrodes in a gas-filled quartz-glass envelope.

dissolve   See **bleed**.

downlight   A light focused vertically downwards – i.e. hitting the stage at 90°.

downstage   The part of the stage nearest to the audience.

FBO   Fade to blackout.

filters   Plastic material placed in front of a light to diffuse it or to colour it by removal of parts of the spectrum. Correction filters adjust the colour temperature to match that of a different light source.

flats   Scenery made in the form of timber frames, traditionally covered with stretched canvas but now more commonly with skin ply.

flicker   Very rapid switching on and off of a light, usually by electronic means.

flood   (1) An instrument which provides a broad wash of light without facilities for adjusting the beam size. (2) Adjust the beam of a spotlight for a wide spread.

fly   Suspend scenery or lights above the stage.

focus spot   Simple instrument which offers control of the emergent conical beam of light by moving lamp and reflector in relation to a fixed planoconvex (PC) lens.

FOH   Front of house, i.e. all spotlights mounted in the auditorium.

found objects   Scenic environment designed from the juxtaposition of existing objects, often not used in a realistic way.

follow spot   Spotlight with which an operator follows an actor's movements on the stage.

Fresnel   A lens where the convex curving front has been broken into a series of steps and the flat rear surface usually has been dimpled to aid diffusion.

gauze   Material woven with a proportion of holes among the thread, varying from the very open net of transformation gauze to the densely woven shark's-tooth gauze. Balance of light in front and behind allows the material to become transparent when required.

gobo   Metal plate with cut-out line image which may be projected by inserting in the gate of a profile spot.

grid   Systematic arrangement of pipes (fixed or on pulleys) for suspending lights and scenery.

HMI   Hygerium metallic iodide: a type of high powered discharge lamp.

instruments   General term for all floodlights, spotlights, beamlights – i.e. devices which house a light source and have facilities for panning, tilting, focusing, etc.

legs   Narrow vertical curtains, usually neutral black, hung for masking purposes.

luminaire   General word for any kind of lighting instrument – i.e. not confined to stage lighting.

masking   Scenery or neutral material placed above and at the sides of the stage to hide the technical areas surrounding the acting area.

minimalism   Staging style based on minimum resources – a term used most frequently in respect of scenery but also applicable to lighting.

multiplex   Digital control signals transmitted from desk to dimmers via a single circuit rather than a separate circuit for each channel.

OP   Opposite prompt side of the stage: actors' right when facing the audience.

open white   A light without a colour filter.

palette   A rig of lighting instruments which have been positioned, coloured and focused to provide a wide range of possibilities for 'painting' the stage with light.

parcan   Simple instrument using a par lamp which includes a fixed optical system within the lamp structure.

PC   See **focus spot**.

practicals   Anything on a stage which actually works rather than merely looking as if it did. Thus lighting 'practicals' are decorative fittings which are capable of being switched on.

primary filters   Deeply saturated filters on red, blue and green.

profile spots   Spotlights which project a hard or soft profile of any two-dimensional shape such as shutters, iris or gobo, placed at the centre ('gate') of the optical system.

PS   Prompt side of the stage: actors' left when facing the audience.

proscenium   The point, often framed, which divides the audience from the stage in a conventional theatre.

Q   Short way of writing 'cue'.

rig   Lights which have been placed in position for a production. 'To rig' is the placing of the lights in these positions.

rostra   Platforms for providing levels on the stage – usually folding to conserve storage space when not in use.

scatter   Stray light outside the main beam, particularly from a Fresnel lens.

smoke gun   Device which produces a non-toxic smoke by vaporizing special fluid.

spill·   Stray light, particularly that emerging from the ventilation holes in a spotlight or from the gap between lens and barndoor. Also light straying outside its intended target – e.g. on to adjacent scenery.

theatre-in-the-round   Staging format where the acting area is surrounded by audience on all sides.

throw   The distance between a lighting instrument and its target.

track   Device for moving scenery in a horizontal plane (e.g. 'tab track' for curtains).

truss   Rigging bars of scaffolding diameter, cross-braced for rigidity.

upstage   The part of the stage furthest from the audience.

variable beam profile spots Profile spotlights where independent movement of a pair of lenses allows a wide range of beam angles with the option of hard or soft edge.

ways The number of control channels in a control system – e.g. a '20-way board'.

wings (1) Space at the side of the stage, beyond the acting area. (2) Scenery, usually in the form of flats positioned at the sides of the stage and normally masking the off-stage areas.

Further reading

Brian Fitt and Joe Thornley, *Lighting Technology*, Focal Press, 1997

David Hays, *Light on the Subject*, Limelight Editions, New York, 1991

Max Keller, *Buhnenbeleuchtung*, Dumont Buchverlag, Cologne, 1985

Richard Pilbrow, *Stage Lighting Design – the Art, the Craft, the Life*, Nick Hern Books, London, and Drama Book Publishers, New York, 1997

Francis Reid, *The ABC of Stage Lighting*, A. & C. Black, London and Drama Book Publishers, New York, 1992

Francis Reid, *The Stage Lighting Handbook*, A. & C. Black, London and Routledge, New York, 1996

Timothy Streader and John A. Williams, *Create Your Own Stage Lighting*, Bell, 1985

Index

Lightning Source UK Ltd.
Milton Keynes UK
UKHW031944151118
332431UK00016B/618/P

9 780240 515458